ERIE SWAMPS

ROAD TRIP TO EDEN

CONNOR FLYNN

BEYOND THE FRAY

Publishing

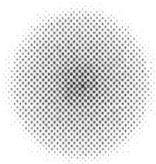

BEYOND THE FRAY

Publishing

"PapPap, is that dog supposed to be walking on two legs?" -
Three years old on the Turner Farm in the Ohio Valley.

CONTENTS

1. Initiation 1
2. Fishing with the Lake Erie Monster 9
3. Crossing the Cry Baby Bridge 17
4. Touching The Witch's Ball 25
5. Sneaking Into Erma's House 33
6. White Shoes 41
7. Escaping Helltown 47
8. Camping with the Ohio Grassman 57
9. October at Mansfield Reformatory 63
10. Surviving Moundsville Prison 69
11. Asheville Castles 77
12. Silver Moon and the Snowman 83
13. Providence Canyon Creatures 91
14. Fishing with the Ocheesee Wild Man 101
15. Midnight at Bellamy Bridge 109
16. Eden Awaits Us 117
17. Final Lap 127
18. Letters From Family and Friends 133

About the Author 155
Also by Connor Flynn 157

CHAPTER 1
INITIATION

Chattahoochee Landing Mounds

C oincidence is the only thing to never exist in this world. My name is Connor the Countryman, and I'll be taking you on a journey from the shores of Lake Erie down to the swamps of the Panhandle. Since I was a young boy, I have always believed in more. And over the years, my path has provided me with what I have needed to see. On our adventure, we'll be exploring campfire stories, crossing cry baby bridges, escaping prison, and hopefully finding the creature in the woods before it finds us. I'm wishing to the stars that our journey ends in Eden, where life began.

This planet is a very strange place and holds many mysteries. The new world has erased our extraordinary past and rewrote our history into a plan more manageable. No matter how many strings they pull and books they burn, the truth's tide has a persistent way of revealing herself when the people need it most. Energy cannot be created or destroyed. It has always existed and is powered by our grand source. We have all been given a battery pack to navigate this plane's terrain. We need to drink more water.

Anomalies and miracles come in many different shapes and forms. We have all experienced déjà vu and reoccurring dreams, but what else is really going on around us? There is a realm of existence that our eyes and ears cannot pick up on. Energy and vibrations surround us, and there are some things that you can only feel. Love, fear, dreaming, and pain. We need to break down the wall of five senses and attempt to become one with the source if we wish to have any answers in this lifetime. We need to cut ties with the burdens that were forced on us since birth. We are free; we always have been.

On our quest for consciousness and enlightenment, we need to remember to navigate with caution. There are many dangers and obstacles that will stand as gatekeepers. The watchers have created a maze of illusion to slow down the ones who seek the eternal flame. The guiding light shines bright, but there are ghouls and goblins along the path. Only follow your soul; only follow your heart.

While adventuring off the grid, please be safe. People are vanishing at alarming rates from national parks and forests every year. The Forest Service is doing a poor job of informing the public of the true danger that is out there. Families deserve to know what lives right down the river from the tent and campsite. Monsters reside in multiple realms… we are all clairvoyant.

Confide in someone you can trust. Tell them where you are going and when you are planning on coming back. They will be the one calling authorities if you don't return by a certain time. Pack extra water or purchase a filter straw if you can. Bring a small first aid kit, food, and a knife. Carry a gun if you know how to use it. And most importantly, buy a personal locator beacon. This could save your life if you go missing.

Make sure to check the weather before you go out. Severe weather and strange phenomena go hand in hand. The water wipes all the tracks away... and the blood too. The predators in the woods plan their attacks around certain weather cycles. Rainstorms, new moons, and full moons are most popular for anomalies. Lock your doors, and please never leave your kids in your car. And I'm not talking about the heat.

People have entered the forest in Pennsylvania and woken up in California fifteen months later. Kids have crawled in caves and met evil versions of their grandparents like in Coraline. Elderly people have been found miles in deep forest where it would have been impossible for them to reach on their own. Thousands of people have claimed they have been abducted by aliens. Weird things are happening and have real-life consequences for the innocent hardworking people of our communities.

Families have had to leave their homestead and go bankrupt for reasons that some people would say don't exist. I'm here to say that ghosts and monsters do exist, and that's no laughing matter. I stand with those innocent people who have been terrorized, misunderstood and ridiculed. It is not fair that good people are forced to be silent. There have been doctors, teachers, truckers, military, policemen, and firemen who all have reported strange occurrences while on duty. It's time we rejoice our fellow man and navigate the old world with our brothers and sisters

4

under the dome. It's up to us to find our own answers.

My quest over the mountains, through the swamps, and across the states remains inward. I have been fasting, experimenting with psychedelics, and trying many different meditation techniques, constantly trying to figure out what configures the twenty-one grams of my soul. My conquest for consciousness began long before I could even pronounce that word. Heaven is a physical place and so is hell. I want to find out the mysteries of the hidden continents. I know I can't legally see the ice wall, but they can't stop my soul from entering the firmament. That's up to my creator.

My journey began when my friends saw Samara in my pantry, when I lost my rod in the Ohio River, and when the giant snake wreaked havoc in the tunnel under my street. I had a terrifying experience while getting my tonsils and adenoids taken out as a youngster that opened me up to the other side. I've been the victim of phantom callers and lost my peace long ago.

I grew up a Boy Scout, farmhand, and avid traveler. Hunting mushrooms and picking berries are hobbies of mine. I chase waterfalls, and I owe it to my cat Baby to find out what lurks in those woods. We found her in my backyard, torn apart by a wild animal. Rest in peace, Baby. I will uncover the truth that has been hidden from us all. I will find your killer.

My mom grew up on a farm, and my dad is a lieutenant fireman. My sister is a lifeguard and survived a coma. My grandpa was a marine, my grandma has Cree blood, and my dad's parents were immigrants from Ireland. My great-aunt saw a banshee more than sixty years ago, and my cousin was tracked by Bigfoot pretty recently. We spent sleepovers listening to the police scanner and crawl space camping. I've had nightmares of the dogman ever since the Sleepy Hollow incident. My family tree was built to withstand the land of the mound builders, but I had a thirst to sink into a new culture.

After twenty-three years, I needed a fresh start down in the swamps of Florida. I drove down to the Sunshine State to referee a flag football tournament and ended up staying long term. I took the passenger seat out of my car and built a bed. I stayed at marinas, state parks, and twenty-four-hour grocery stores. I survived by timing when the market disposed of their extra fruit and vegetables. When you follow your destined path, your needs and desires will be met in abundance. But when you are on the road, you have to watch out for creatures crossing the street and entities trying to hitch a ride.

I made a Couchsurfing account and ended up staying with a band. I ended up moving in with them and managing their punk rock musical. It had magical potions and witches, so it was right up my alley! We performed all over the state, and I was really thrown into the DIY folk culture. It was perfect for what I was looking for. We meditated daily, learned how to screen print, and I soaked up many things about crystals, spirits and my soul.

After Hurricane Irma struck, I moved toward the Panhandle to be closer to my mom's farm. I got a job at the local bowling alley and moved into a trailer. I felt like a king to have my own roof. I spent a lot of time biking to my mom's ranch, picking fruit and playing with the animals. She has a couple of gardens and an awesome fishing pond. Though, thanks to Bly Manor, I'm terrified of it. But we couldn't imagine some of the horrors that awaited us as we pranced through paradise in the months before October.

The worst storm to ever make landfall in the country struck our town directly. Cyclones and strong winds ripped my trailer apart, but luckily I evacuated to my mom's. She lost most of her trees, and the land was forever reshaped, but luckily we were intact. When the storm's eye passed over our yard, it was psychedelic. The alley was destroyed. Many people lost their lives, and almost everybody was emotionally traumatized. But one thing about the human spirit is that it's very durable, and we will bounce back. I believe that begins with the truth.

This is a collection of my notes, journals, and data that I have been working on since before the millennium.

I remember the craze about Y2K, watching United 93 fly right over my school, and reports of all the UFO activity around Lake Erie. I grew up researching haunted houses and Bigfoot during my free time, so it's only appropriate I take my fellow truthers down the rabbit hole of discovery and consciousness.

Along my journey I have gathered a collection of evidence that may surprise even the greatest of skeptics. We have pictures of mysterious scat, tree formations, and large orbs. We have photographed footprints and recorded loud hoots. Not many people have had the opportunity to hold remnants of our ancestors, but I held a giant metacarpal thumb bone in my own two hands, so I have no time for people who claim there is no evidence.

The people running this world have just an incredible job of sweeping the truth under a rug. This will be an adventure of recovering our lost legends and locating our hidden history. Please follow me on a road trip through time and matter from the banks of South Bay down to the Emerald Coast as I retrace my steps navigating mysteries of my past. Beware of the tall deer, and toast before you sip from the Fountain of Youth.

CHAPTER 2
FISHING WITH THE LAKE ERIE MONSTER

LAKE ERIE

Hockey, beer, and cryptids. Sure sounds like a usual Friday night for me, but I'm actually talking about the Lake Erie Monster. With sightings going back to the 1800s and many human disappearances pointed in her direction, Bessie has made quite the name for herself. The year I was born, three fishermen were found dead, and soon after there was a $100,000 bounty for a creature at least thirty feet long in the South Bay. There have been many shipwrecks, UFO sightings, mysterious drownings, and tales of deep caves below the lake that could be linked closely to this mythical creature and her family.

Many years ago, a fisherman was on the bank and saw a couple of rats running on some rocks. He threw a rock towards them, and a large creature barreled into the water. Many other witnesses have reported seeing a cigar-shaped serpent anywhere from thirty to sixty feet long. A family sailboat was attacked, and it made national news. There was even a replica of the monster made and displayed in a Cleveland museum. She has been spotted by Canadians as well.

Growing up, I spent a lot of time on Lake Erie. From the Edgewater Summers, Cedar Point HalloWeekends, to walking on the ice during winter, I was always on the water. I spent a few Saturday nights on the docks near the Rock & Roll Hall of Fame. We would spend all night around a garbage-can fire, playing cards and telling stories before the Browns game the next day. There was a fleet of boats cheering on the orange and brown with their radios and mini TVs on the waves right outside the stadium. It's quite the experience roaring with the crowd. But what sticks out more is the tales I heard on the docks.

A retired fireman mentioned sightings of eels, bull sharks, and even stingrays. He went on and on about the Erie Marlin, aka the Saileye. The air-breathing bowfin and vampire lamprey were cool, but the one that I was fascinated by was bigger than his boat. The fisherman said his life changed when he was pulled overboard by some kind of monster. He was able to cut his hand free after being dragged under water for at least twenty feet. He said it had to be either a giant sturgeon or the beast from below.

We all heard the stories about the Loch Ness cousin that roamed the dark water. I still remember googling it with classmates and seeing the newspaper clipping of Bessie sinking ships. The most documented story described how more than sixty seamen witnessed two plesiosaur creatures fighting up near Toledo. If there's two, there's plenty. I knew there was something to the legend.

I went to many of my dad's flag football tournaments as a young boy. We visited Chicago, DC, Pittsburgh, Buffalo, Columbus, and Orlando. But my favorite tourney was the referees cup right on Lake Erie. The fields were right on the water, and there were plenty of trails for adventuring. The amazing scenery always inspired a mountain of stories and legends from my dad's teammates. They lured me in with their tall tales, and I have been hooked ever since!

A group of us kids would always go exploring along the edge of the lake. Some wanted to escape for a cigarette, but I was always down for seeing new things. The urban guys would warn us younger boys not to get too close to the water or Bessie will get us. Down on that sand was the first place I ever had to use my sock for toilet paper. Down on that sand was the first time I ever saw a kid go to the bathroom in his pants.

We wandered endlessly down the coastline. Hopping from rock to rock. Cement block to wherever we could stand. The waves crashed at our feet as we searched for shells and dead fish. We grabbed onto logs and launched them into the water. We threw rocks up into the bank and screamed to the abyss. We were kids being kids. The kings of the summer.

The smell of dead fish always attracted a crowd. We all covered our mouths and pushed each other near the carcass. One kid grabbed a stick and picked up the fish and started running after us. Then another kid started screaming. He wasn't afraid of the stanky fish. He was pointing toward the water.

By the time I turned my head, there was nothing to be seen, but I could clearly see a disturbance in the water. The boy kept saying it was a giant snake. Of course, the adults said it was a sturgeon. But from the sheer terror in the kid's voice, I guarantee he saw a monster. The rest of our hikes over the next few years centered around catching another glimpse of the beast.

A decade later, I was working at Family Video and met a competitive fisherman named Root. He offered to take me out on his charter to catch some walleye with his crew. We spent the night before in a trailer beside the water. We caught dinner, and they told me some stories. They laughed when I mentioned sharks, but all had their own take on giant sturgeon. Each and every one of them had had a rod or two broken from something down there.

We got our equipment set up and called it a night. I went to my room and saw all the pictures of the monster fish that these guys had caught over the years. I went to sleep dreaming of trophy fish, but in my nightmares was the Lake Erie Monster.

I woke up early and smoked a joint beside the water, imagining the hidden treasure and mystery below. I tossed the roach in the water for sacrifice and good fortune. I closed my eyes and tried to conjure some ancient energy of the Great Lakes. I thought deep about the ancient, unearthed structures of an advanced civilization, the salt mines below, and the queen herself, Bessie's dream. There was a feeling in the air that I couldn't explain. There was a sense of sonic energy like a dolphin using echolocation to communicate with me. The feeling stuck with me on the boat ride out toward Canada to deeper waters.

After hours of catching a couple of hundred perch, some monster walleye and pike, that feeling had come back. The water had become a little darker, and the wind began to pick up. There was mist blanketing the distance and a drizzle from above. The waves were crashing into our boat, and I knew we were no longer alone. It was starting to look like we should be heading back when Root's rod began to bend. He held on for dear life and finally strapped into his rod. His crew attached his belt to a metal hook on the floor of the boat. He wasn't going anywhere. Then suddenly another pole bent over, and within seconds I was in the belt and strapped to the floor. I watched Root out of the corner of my eye and synced into his rhythm, fighting our beasts.

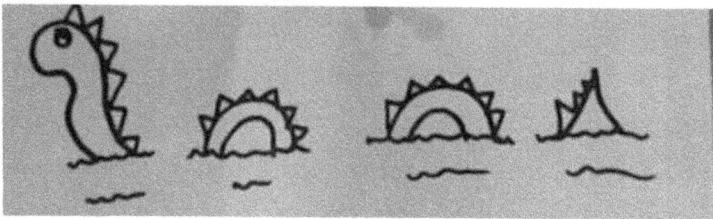

Bessie (The South Bay Serpent)

After twenty exhausting minutes, the rain picked up, and we had a decision to make. It was starting to get dangerous, and we had a long ride back home. Root came up with a more aggressive tactic of reeling. We began to make ground on our fish, but suddenly we felt a hard knock on the boat. We all went falling back on deck and jumped up with wide eyes, peering overboard. Root put even more muscle into his rod, and suddenly his line snapped. I knew what was coming next, so I took my knife out and cut my line. I stared into the water while the guys judged me from behind. In the distance, a snakelike creature launched parallel with the water, shining in the moonlight. As its tail flicked in the water, I now knew that life was much stranger than they were telling us.

CHAPTER 3

CROSSING THE CRY BABY BRIDGE
VALLEY CITY, OHIO

O hio soil is rich with history. The Cleveland area is plagued with haunted castles, bad luck, and roads that go nowhere. The fire at the Gore Orphanage, Melonheads, and the Loveland Frogmen are just the tip of the iceberg. Down 71 South, when you leave the bright lights of downtown, you head right into the darkness, and that's where I grew up. October was always my favorite month for all the scary movies and free candy, but our neighborhood had tales of real witches and pure evil that kept us on the prowl all year long…

In kindergarten, I remember riding the cheese with all the sixth graders. These kids were smoking and making out in the back of the bus while I was only five years old, still watching *Timmy the Tooth*. Luckily the neighbor girls, Chrissy and Lid, looked out for me. But because of that, I sat with the older kids. Chrissy put me by the window next to Lid and told me to keep quiet. I remember this badass kid named Stanley, who was always causing trouble for the driver and bringing his new girlfriends home twice a week. He listened to metal, rode a dirt bike, and drew twisted dark comics. That's where I first heard about Cry Baby Bridge.

Stanley drew a picture of a girl who looked like Samara from *The Ring*. The woman was standing on a railroad bridge, about fifty feet up, with a church in the background. She was holding her baby, but not in a loving way; she was about to drop it. It was a shocking picture, yes. But it had my attention because I'd seen that place before. And it was just a couple of streets from my house… And from the school, our bus route is closest, and out of the route, my house and Stanley's were on the nearest corner. So of course, when Stan told his stories, he always made sure the girls and I could hear. He would sing, "She killed her baby; then she killed herself. They called her crazy; she jumped to Hell!" over and over.

I remember being so scared of the old dying sister in the original *Pet Sematary* that I had to talk to my doctor about it. I still have a vivid memory of a dream of her chasing me around the tree we used to wait for the school bus at. Looking back, it probably had something to do with the real-life terror right down the railroad. My bed would shake at night while the train rode by, and I couldn't tell if I was awake or dreaming, shivering scared of this demon lady. That shit still gives me the creeps, typing this in the dark halfway across the country. I felt true fear for a brief moment when her character was introduced in the remake.

Stan brought up a couple of kids who went missing a few years before that. He said, "The witch got them, or the Graveyard did. Either way, they went over that bridge." He called the church the "Graveyard" because beside the church was a cemetery, and he said that's where all the real services took place. Stan told us that when he went out there with his older brother, they saw red lights inside the windows and heard baby cries before being chased off by one of the church people. He said that they were always watching and were always looking for new members.

Years later, my family was having a cookout with some old friends, and naturally the campfire brought out some spooky stories. After a couple of *Light as a feather, Stiff as a board* stories, my mom's best friend brought up the Cry Baby Bridge and started pointing toward my mom. My mom started to embarrassingly smile and waited for Cris to get on with the story while she died inside as the clock ticked.

In what felt like a lifetime later for my mom, Cris revealed that they went out there with a couple of boys in high school and parked right under the bridge. The group got out of the car, smoked a joint, wandered up the hill and through the cemetery. But when they returned to the car, it wouldn't start. And there were fingerprints all over the windows and chips in the paint of the fancy ride. Most of the party didn't believe the story, but I did. And I knew I would have to go check it out for myself.

Months later, it was football season, and I was playing on the Browns with all my best friends. I came from the Chargers, and this was my first year as tackle on the new team. The team was known for winning and had traditions on and off the field. At one of the first team meetings, I heard the varsity kids talking about the annual haunted house tour. They were talking about hayrides and the world-famous "7 Floors of Hell". But I had a different suggestion... They laughed at first, but my buddy Adam from the bus was on the Browns and brought up Stan, and they shut up real quick. Couple of weekends later, it was Halloween and time to get spooky. We passed out candy and then hit up the Scream Park. After escaping the Catacombs and the clown house, we planned on hitting a couple of real haunts.

We all piled in the station wagon and headed into the boonies. The excitement turned into fear when we turned onto Abbeyville Road. We could feel it in the air; we felt like we were at the edge of the world. All of a sudden, Richie slammed on the brakes, put the car in park, and ran out of the car with the keys in the ignition. He shouted for everyone to follow him out of sight. We hesitated but finally caught up after he called again. We found him around the bend and started fussing, wondering what just happened. He shushed us and calmly walked back toward the car. All the headlights were now off, and we all started to really panic. A few seconds later, we saw headlights approaching and ran as fast as we could toward the car. We hopped in the first door that we could and started screaming, "Go, go, go!" but the engine was skipping. Richie, now terrified and pumping the gas, finally got the wagon started. He burned rubber while this huge truck came screaming at us with his horn blaring like *Jeepers Creepers*. We took a quick left and turned up the hill and into the "Church" and parked near the cemetery.

Adam and I looked at each other and wondered what we'd gotten ourselves into. But the surreal feeling of living out a comic book kept us moving forward. We explored the exterior of the church and saw the red lights that I'd heard so much about. The air was filled with mist, and we followed the winding path between the graves. It felt like there were shadows and faces watching us at every turn. We dipped off into the woods until we reached the railroad tracks and headed back toward the bridge.

I lost myself in a daze of walking, and the next thing I knew, there was no more ground between the railroad ties. I was about fifty feet up above the road in a thick cloud of fog. I would have never made it that far if I had been paying attention (I still haven't been out that far since). The wind felt good, and the sounds of nature were peaceful when I closed my eyes to listen for the cries. But after a few seconds of serenity, my knees began to rumble, and I heard whistling through the trees. There was something wrong, but I was frozen. There was a train coming, and I was the closest one to it. The crew's *Stand By Me* screams brought me back to consciousness, and I hustled back, trying not to plummet to my death. The conductor saw us and laid on the horn. We dove off the side about fifteen feet down into the dirt and rolled back down to the street.

After the roller coaster of chills and thrills, we headed

back toward the car and saw something unexpected in the parking lot. It was the truck from before, but it was now empty. We looked around, paranoid, and ran toward the buggie. I took one last look in the church windows and scanned the misty headstones before hopping in the car. Richie opened his door, just standing there staring. We rushed him until we noticed what was slowing him down.

There was a slice of chocolate cake on a red plate with a fork sitting on the driver's seat. I didn't understand until Joey said, "Devil's cake," and Richie threw it on the ground and started the car. He peeled down the hill, and I could have sworn I saw the truck lights turn back on. I kept quiet, and we all didn't say a word until we reached town. We pulled into the drive and dapped up. Joey told us, "Maybe next time we will get to see Erma's house," and Richie said, "And the Witch's Ball too!" After winning the championship that season, we never saw those guys again, but that night laid the foundation for my interest in nocturnal sightseeing.

CHAPTER 4
TOUCHING THE WITCH'S BALL
MYRTLE HILL CEMETERY

There are witches in every country of the world. Most don't ride brooms and wear pointy hats; they are dressed as normal people. They are mothers, nurses, teachers and usually beautiful in appearance. The women from Eastwick and Salem are just the tip of the iceberg Some believe that Eve was a witch, and others pointed fingers at Jesus's mother, Mary. There have been plenty of curses and spells over the years, but many witches are healers and prophetesses as well.

The Sanderson sisters and the girls from *The Craft* are an interesting look into the world of witches, but my favorite is Thomasin in the old New England colonial days. The chilling story shows that even innocent daughters can be lured into the dark underworld. Many women summon Marie Laveau and Morgan le Fay during the spooky season. The Bell Witch and Pungo Witch legends have always plagued the Appalachian region, but the Witch's Ball is closest to my court.

Billy's dad lived across from Myrtle Hill Cemetery. The front window peered right into the gateway entrance. We would stay up all night, playing *Devil May Cry* and *WWE Here Comes The Pain*, tracking the activity of the graveyard. JJ's friends would come over for PPV events and often tell us stories about the haunted cemetery and its most famous attraction, the Witch's Ball. The large granite sphere was placed on the Stoskopf gravesite to prevent the witch from rising from the dead.

There are various tellings of the story that intertwine with other stories of murder and witchcraft in the area, but most take shape around some common themes. A woman had been left by her husband and then was ridiculed by her family and the public, slowly being driven toward insanity. She hosted a party, and her visitors were poisoned. Her family was stuffed in a well in the backyard, and the woman was found with enough arsenic to kill the rest of the town. She was hunted down by the townspeople and sentenced to death. Cults and ghost hunters flock the grave during the witching hour, trying to summon Stoskopf and finally free her from Myrtle Hill. Her victims were buried nearby, and their cries can be heard through the trees.

For Bill's birthday, a group of us ordered pizza and rented scary movies from Hollywood Video. After hours of fun, and when JJ went to bed, some of us snuck out and into the cemetery. We took our time creeping in the shadows before making it over to the ball. The ball was known to be warm in the winter and almost too cold to touch in the summer. Jay's friends said rain and snow would never fall on it.

We each touched the ball and marveled at the moonlight beaming off of the stone. Headlights pulled in, and we all scattered. The car quickly killed the lights and cruised through the cemetery in the dark. They parked near the building and got out of the car, dressed in all black. I hid behind a gravestone and luckily had an eye on a couple of my friends.

Orb captured at Witch's Ball

The lucky few made it back across the street. But JT, Hink, and I had suspicious activity between us and safety. The group in black lit candles and sat around the ball. When they started chanting, we knew it was our time to go. We slid between gravestones, peeking back at their enormous swaying shadows being projected on the pine trees in the distance.

Energy Overload

The wind began to pick up as we headed towards the woods to cross at a safe distance. But a loud tree crack from the abyss sent us running back toward the ball. The candles were out, and the group was nowhere to be found. The three of us sat with our backs against the tallest tree. JT had had enough. He just bolted toward the house with no regard for us left behind. Hink took off once he saw that JT made it to the garage. I sat there paralyzed, trying to map out a safe route. My life flashed in front of my eyes. I envisioned myself back on Boston Road, running through my backyard while my dad cut the grass. My mom yelled my name…

Late night investigation

I visualized escaping the cemetery, only to be run over by a speeding car crossing the street. I was interrupted when I felt something crawling on me; it was a spider. I stood up, swatted it off, and a couple of twigs and leaves fell from above. I looked up, and something dark and deformed was crawling down after me. I ran as fast as I could as the cries rang through the tall pillar graves. I ran and dove into the safe haven of needed space.

We were covered in bruises and cuts from our necks down to our feet. Luckily Bill's dad moved the next winter, but I returned many times to see what was going on at the Myrtle Hill Cemetery. The grounds are a very popular destination for my fever dreams and dehydration nightmares...

CHAPTER 5

SNEAKING INTO ERMA'S HOUSE

ABBEVILLE ROAD

W e stopped at the Witch's Ball and drove under the Cry Baby Bridge, but tonight was about Erma's house. We turned off Abbeville Road and parked not far from the famous church in the complete darkness. We then trekked down 167 until it dead-ended. The walk was along the Rocky

River, and it masked the sound of us pretty well. We explained to the girls that another mother had gone crazy and killed her family. They say she sent her family down the coal chute before hanging herself in the attic. Beware of the pale door. To reach the Garden of God, we must first pass the Blair Witch.

Many tales link the nearby cry baby bridges and local disappearances to the house, but we were gonna find out for ourselves very soon. The road descended under a canopy of thick trees, and that was when we knew we were getting close. It got much darker as we crept past a couple of houses close to the road that were unavoidable on our path. We moved in silence, trying not to alarm the neighbors and their animals.

Erma's house was the last house on the right. But before the haunt, we had to survive the one on the left. A sign covered in bullet holes gave us a clear picture of how they felt about trespassers, so we moved with caution. But swiftly, because the owner of the house was known to sic his dogs on the ones who were not welcome. As we approached the end of the street, the safest place was inside the house.

The white house was covered in graffiti, and most of the windows were broken. I scanned them for faces and made sure everyone was with me. The time was now, and there was no going back. There were five of us, so we would have to move quickly for us not to be spotted.

We had our eyes on the cellar, and they all followed behind, pushing me in the back, barging through the entrance. We pulled out our flip phone flashlights and saw appliances and garbage spread in every direction. Squatters had definitely been living there. We moved toward the stairs, but all halted when we thought we heard some movement on the floorboards above our head.

The girls wanted to scatter, but I kept moving forward because inside the house was probably still the safest spot. We crept up the steps, and I led the way with my flashlight. A few stairs were missing, and the rest were wobbly, so the higher we climbed, the more dangerous it was. I made it up to the main floor and scanned the nearby area with my light.

The kitchen was trashed, with dishes and utensils scattered in every direction. People had definitely been staying there... recently. I helped my friends up, and we walked into the living room. The furniture was torn apart and thrown around the room. The floor was covered in Christmas cards and letters addressed to Alma.

After getting to know the family through the Christmas cards, we moved slowly toward the murder site. We moved slowly upstairs and huddled in the master bedroom. There was a wooden beam that ran from one end of the room to the other. That was where Erma tied a rope and hung herself after she killed her family. There was an eerie feeling in that room. We searched around for missing clues and were floored when we discovered the hatch to the coal chute.

We opened it up and listened for anything suspicious. It sounded like a cry, so I stuck my head farther in, and before I got a chance to listen again, a swarm of bats blew past me and headed for the holes in the window. It caused quite a commotion, and we began to hear the dogs barking. We woke the neighbors. Getting back to our car wasn't going to be an easy stroll.

The group was scared of being killed, but I was more nervous about going to jail. We peeked through the windows and saw a man with a flashlight heading toward the house with a pack of his guard dogs. I knew we all wouldn't make it if we traveled together, so I came up with a plan.

I told Skotko that I'd meet them in the car. He knew I would be the decoy and shook my hand, saying, "Just like *Halo*." I busted down the back door and took off running into the woods. The dogs caught a glimpse of me and were right on my tail, barking up a storm. The rest of my group waited patiently in the cellar for a window of opportunity to escape.

I made it to the shadows, crossed the road, and slid down the steep cliffs into the creek. The man and dogs followed into the darkness. The rest of the group took off toward the car while the man scanned the valley, searching for me. I ran out of darkness and was stuck under a ledge. I held my breath like Frodo hiding from Nazgul in *The Lord of the Rings*. The man was so close, I could smell the rank scent of his dirty clothes and also heard him say, "I'm going to kill these kids," while loading his shotgun. I remained silent, and after a while, he took off back toward the road and, sadly, my group.

I made it back to the shadows and began worrying about my friends. I knew there was a slim chance that he could intercept them, and it could all turn much worse. I couldn't take the risk. I started to make noise, and the dogs came hounding. I saw the flashlight turn in my direction, and I knew he had seen me.

I took off on the hillside and felt it before I had heard it. It felt like I was on fire, but I was not going to let those dogs tear me apart. I imagined him capturing me and taking me back to his house like in the movie *Wolf Creek*. I figured I would much rather die running than being tortured by this backwoods bosh.

A couple more shots rang out, colliding with the stone cliffside surrounding me. I was covered in leaves, dirt and blood. He fired one final shot, and I dove off a ledge as it hit near my feet. I went tumbling headfirst into the raging river. I kept my head under water and made it to the other side. I climbed up to the road and circled back toward the car.

My friends were relieved to see me. After they heard all the shotgun blasts, they thought that they would be heading back to town without me. But instead, they helped pick the shrapnel out of my leg and shoulder. We made it home safely and spent the night at Southwick. We went up to the gas station for a late-night snack and heard some kids who had just seen a ghost named "White Shoes".

CHAPTER 6
WHITE SHOES
SOUTHWICK MANOR WOODS

Southwick Manor Squad (Left to right: Billy, Lavelle, Hinkle)

spent many nights in Southwick Manor. After football games, I'd sleep over at Patrick's and always get into mischief. He was a couple of years older and loved pulling pranks around the neighborhood. After he moved out, Hinkle's was the spot to be at.

We played video games and collected football cards. But when Billy's mom moved in near the basketball court, our crew swarmed and took over the basement. Then Lavelle moved in next door, and our team was complete.

With multiple TVs, we played in *Halo* tournaments and made ninja videos. We recorded over a hundred songs and would walk to Speedway and McDonald's for entertainment. We called ourselves "The Storm", but the tennis coach called us goons when we would all walk to practice through the woods. Those were some of the best times of my life. For many Southwick was just a dead-end street, but for my crew, it was everything we ever needed.

After a full day of running hoops, we decided to play Manhunt. We recruited all of our friends from the presidential streets and rich neighborhood to square off against the goon squad of the low-income apartment complex. Stars from the high school football team, theater actresses, and the dropouts all came to play. We put stripes on our faces and wore all black and camo like we were in *Splinter Cell*. We all met up on the basketball court to discuss the rules and collect the dues. One person was randomly picked to hide, and the rest of the players would search the surrounding area and need to tag the target to end the game. Everybody put in a dollar, and the winner would take all. There were side bets and everything. After a few minutes of discussion, I was the chosen one to be hunted.

I ran off into the woods with a couple-minute head start. My heart was pumping. It really felt like I would be killed if I was discovered. My plan was to get far enough away from the base to force them to spread out. Then I would sneak past them in the shadows and find a spot near the HQ. I ran for a couple of minutes and made it to the tunnel creek. The noise of the rushing water was able to drown out the sound of my heavy breathing and heart pumping. I relaxed for a bit and took cover in the tube when I heard the older kids screaming, "We gonna find you. We gon' hurt you…"

I peeked through the brush and saw a group of hunters flipping over logs and splashing rocks into the water less than ten feet from where I was crouched. I was able to slip past them, and after a couple of minutes of stealth, I could see light peeking through the trees.

I creeped through the parking lot, hiding behind cars, and realized I was behind the bowling alley. I heard something in the woods, and while I was peeking back, I crashed into something. It was a person, a big woman in a coat. She was walking towards the building next door; it was Alcoholics Anonymous. She went smashing down on the ice, and I was frightened that I had accidentally killed her. I rushed to see if she was alright, and when I made it over to her, she was laughing. I helped her up and told her I was playing hide-and-seek with my friends.

Before I got a chance to ask her if she knew any spots, she was leading me on my way. She told me that she used to play in these same woods and knew a spot where I would never be found. I followed behind close and was led into a small camp. There were license plates, movie theater chairs, and many other pieces of town that were put together to create this small colony.

We sat down within the walls, and she handed me a snack. The woman told me a story about a girl who was left neglected while her father would get drunk at the bowling alley. The girl was forced to stay near the parking lot and was not allowed to pass the fence. On the other side, the children were playing and having fun, but she could not join. She would peek around the corner, but most of the time, all that could be seen were her white shoes.

After one long night at the bar, her father wrecked his car on the way home. The young girl was killed, and the father was arrested. He did his time and was forced to attend AA meetings... ironically right next door. The father would cry and tell his story every week. Months later, he relapsed and crashed his car again. He was killed, and the family tree had reached its end. Or so they thought...

That was when I had a flashback of Pat's sister telling

us the story of the ghost near the playground. I remembered her describing the white shoes. I remembered the older kids teasing when the ball rolled to the trees. And like it was a dream, the lady went on to tell me that the young girl still waits beside the fence, listening to the laughter, anticipating her chance to finally play.

I listened to a couple more stories and lost track of time. I snapped out of my trance when I heard the call of "Olly olly oxen free!" and thanked the woman for her kind hospitality before heading through the woods. She gave me a rope necklace, and I left her my Tamagotchi. I approached the fence and slowly went to peek around the corner. But before I turned my neck, I heard a soft voice say, "You won".

I didn't even bother to turn around before replying, "I wish you could have played too." She whispered, "I'm always part of the game." I felt a breeze of wind and knew she was back in heaven, swimming in the waters of the Firmament. I smiled and made my way around the fence. I hope to be reunited with her one day. Maybe in Eden... The crowd mistook me with legend and yelled, "White Shoes," and finally, I understood what she meant. I smiled and asked the group why they couldn't find me. And every time I walked past, I would toss a coin or two over the fence to my guardian angel.

CHAPTER 7
ESCAPING HELLTOWN
BOSTON MILLS, OHIO

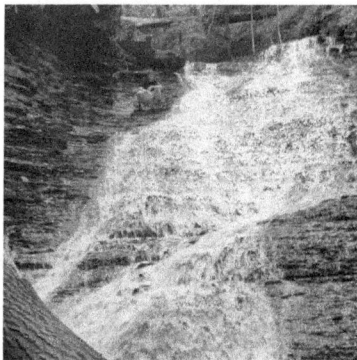

Cuyahoga Valley National Park. Home of the
Grassman.

After a night in Helltown, Vegas was a breeze. Sin City has its own type of creatures, but I think I would still prefer to take my chances with the ones with giant claws and teeth. On our adventure to Eden, it only makes sense to pass the gates of fire.

The waterfalls and ski resorts lure the friendly folk into the winding cliffs of Peninsula, but the headless horseman on the highway to hell makes sure they are never to find their way out. There are rumors of a chemical spill that mutated the wildlife, deep tunnels, and even an abandoned mansion scattered across the dense remains of the real-life Silent Hill. Watch where you step; many bodies have been dumped in Helltown... You don't want to be another one.

Growing up playing *Resident Evil* and *Silent Hill*, my babysitter would tell me about the real-life place called Helltown. He told me that mutated people hid in caves like *The Hills Have Eyes* and that there was hidden treasure that kept people coming back regardless of the danger. I was on the fence about it all until my parents told me about an *X-Files* episode about it, and I knew I had to check it out. Years went on, and I heard more and more stories. A couple that come to mind were satanic racists burning crosses, horrifying war records, and the tale of the famous Peninsula Python, the giant snake that led an escape of exotic animals from the circus that leaked into the local ecosystem.

After too long on the outskirts, I finally had a full day lined up to explore Helltown. During the day, I was to explore and scout with my good friend Bird, while Wolf was at home preparing for our overnight camp and ghost hunt. Bird is like a brother to me, and his nickname somewhat relates to his real name. Wolf, on the other hand, is actually part wolf. I believe him when he claims that he has turned into one in deep meditation and actually has found fur after he came back to. He also had a gun and some pretty cool tactical equipment that took the hunt to the next level.

We started the day off at Brandywine Falls and quickly linked up with a group of local adventurers. We smoked and skipped rocks for a while and then started down the creek. Abe led the way and made sure to find each of us a hiking stick. He showed us his blade, and when one of the girls questioned him, he took off his shirt and showed us a huge scar across his back. A mountain lion had attacked him. It wasn't the first time I had heard of big cats in the area. There were panthers, puma, jags, and cougars. I've heard stories about the *Black Cat* all my life. If a man who could kill me with his bare hands felt the need to carry a weapon, I knew I'd be not taking any chances later tonight. I picked up a sharp rock and put it in my pocket just in case.

Abe showed us some unmarked graves, took us to the dump yard, and told us he knew where some caves were. I couldn't help but think about my babysitter's bedtime stories, but I'd rather do it in the daylight than at midnight with the werewolf. We found the caves but couldn't go too far without the proper equipment. But they were clearly deep, and there was no telling what could be lurking below. One of Abe's friends, Cole, had a theory, saying, "The caves go all the way down to hell, and the Grim Reaper himself is waiting right past that ledge." We headed back to the hills.

After a couple of hours, we smelled a horrible stench in the air. Abe then told us about the slaughterhouse and led us up to an abandoned barn. I couldn't tell if I was just woozy coming down from the smoke, or that shit was beginning to get serious. We explored the area until the girls claimed they felt like they were being watched. I thought that maybe it was a ghost or the Grassman, but Abe and his crew were on high alert from there on out, ready for whatever it was.

We made it back to civilization and said our good-byes. They recommended we don't pick up hitchhikers and to check out the Mother of Sorrows Cemetery next time we were back. Little did they know, we would be back sooner than I could list all the monsters reported here. We just didn't want to mention anything because for all we knew Abe and his crew could go *Last House on the Left* on us!

On the ride home we listened to Pink Floyd and The Doors as the sun went down. We were deep in a trance when a deer ran out in front of us. Luckily, Bird swerved out of the way, and we laughed about it when we got home and smoked a blunt. Soon after, he left, and I fell asleep on the couch. I was back in town and passing the famous gas station. I was on foot, and I felt that something was after me. I turned around and caught a glimpse of something emerging from the hillside mist. My feet felt like I was stuck in thick mud. I was sinking and couldn't get away. A hearse emerged from the smoke and was not slowing down. It was going to run me over. I fought through the muck and jumped into the ditch while the funeral van went crashing into the tree beside me. I closed my eyes and went into the fetal position like a bear was about to attack me.

There was a knock on the door, and my nightmare had ended. Wolf was on my porch, and I knew it was time to head back into Hell. His girlfriend was waiting in the car. Her name was Gwen, and it was the first time I had met her. She was really pretty and had some interesting tattoos and piercings. I could tell she was artistic and had a deeper side to her. "Rhiannon" by Fleetwood Mac came on the radio, and she transformed. She sang with full emotion, and after the performance, she revealed her mother was a Wiccan and that she was actually named after the first woman hanged for witchcraft, Gwen ferch Ellis. She had been studying Wicca and the moon cycles for nearly her entire life. Tonight would be a full moon and a perfect night to do some ritual practice. She handed me a crystal and explained the five elements of the pentagram. We finished the ride with some chants and a sip of wine. When we arrived and parked, she lit a candle and carried it up the path to the abandoned graveyard.

Abandoned graveyard

After a steep climb in the pitch black, we arrived at an opening in the tree line. The candle flickered, went out, and Gwen said, "We're here." We walked the perimeter of the cemetery, and Wolf pointed his flashlight into the woods, showing us some hidden gravestones. He also said that the surrounding trees have been said to come to life and whisper to nocturnal visitors. There was a certain headstone that a ghost was known to sit on, but he must have been up on his feet while we were there. Gwen had relit the candle and had us sit in a circle around it. We began to hum and watch the flame take life. The wind began to pick up, and there was certainly some activity around us. Their energy was intoxicating. The vibrations brought strong visualizations and inward feelings. The hums climaxed, and the storm of emotion came to a sudden halt when we opened our eyes.

After capturing some giant orbs on camera, we trekked down the mound and back into the heart of the forest. I was looking backward, listening to one of Gwen's stories, and almost fell on my face. I thought it was a tree root that I had tripped over. But I jumped back in shock when the thing started to move. I hopped away and shrieked when I saw that it was a snake the size of me! Wolf and Gwen laughed and didn't seem too bothered. They said, "That's just a baby. They get five times that size!" I was on high alert from there on out. After about an hour of exploring, we saw a giant structure ahead of us. I thought it was another abandoned house, but it was actually a school bus! And when I looked closer, it looked like someone was in there. It looked like they were smoking a cigarette.

Wolf noticed the shadow and called out to them. The shadow ducked down, and we approached the bus, ready to rumble. Wolf announced that he had a gun and did not want any problems. We opened up the door and peeked our heads inside. The bus was empty but definitely still smelled like cigarettes. We searched all the seats, and there was no trace of the rider. But Gwen did find a nice Zippo lighter with a weird symbol on it. We used that to light up a joint and slowly descended into the darkness of Hell. After twenty intense minutes of group meditation, we were interrupted by gunshots. We knew it was time to get back to the car...

I wondered if it was maybe Abe and his crew, but I did not plan on waiting around for confirmation. Wolf and Gwen moved like Bonnie and Clyde, sneaking from tree to tree for cover. I followed a safe distance behind, just in case they were ambushed. I was sweating bad, and the bugs were attacking me wherever my skin was bare. In a daze, I wondered if they were target shooting, exchanging gunfire, or protecting themselves from predators.

I got part of my answer when we heard multiple people screaming and yelling. They were not shooting targets or each other. They sounded worried. They were being hunted. Now I was beginning to wonder if we should stop running from the noise and maybe head toward it for some assistance. Wolf was set on getting Gwen to safety, so our mission was pretty clear. We reached the car and were caught in the crossroads. Gwen knew we were torn at heart and told us to go see if we could help. She gave me a flare gun and told me to aim high. We took off down the trail, and not a minute later, we heard something coming right towards us.

We heard it trampling toward us, and before we were attacked, I shot the flare gun. The orange beam of light illuminated the forest, and we finally saw what was making that noise. It wasn't a monster, but they were running from one. It was two men, and crazily enough, I recognized them. I pushed Wolf's gun down, but he raised it back up to cover them as they passed. Before hearing a word, I followed Abe and Cole, hightailing it out of the darkness. We finally made it to the car, and Abe started spazzing out about a group of hooded figures trying to abduct them. I'd had enough *Eyes Wide Shut* for the day, so I was ready to go. Abe gave me a hug and said he thought he would never see me again. He did the same to Gwen? What a weird day in Helltown...

CHAPTER 8
CAMPING WITH THE OHIO GRASSMAN

SALT FORK, OHIO

Old sketch of Ohio Grassman

unters, moonshiners, and even other Bigfoot aren't safe from the Ohio Grassman. With sightings from Helltown down to the Ohio River, this rogue Sasquatch has been wreaking havoc across the Buckeye State since before the Native Americans were here. A new breed known to be bigger and much more curious and violent than our furry friend Harry Henderson, the Grassman sees no problem challenging bears, approaching campsites, and ruining moonshine stills. In the land of giants, a war before time may have led to the Grassman's being cast away and created a new branch to the tree of mysteries in the Double O.

The Buckeye soil is home to sacred grounds. There are over ten thousand mounds throughout the state. Giant skeletons have been excavated from mammoth caves in Toledo, near the Serpent Mound in Peebles, and in many places along the Ohio River. The sun worshippers were buried in a sitting position facing east. In Chillicothe, they found a king and queen buried with silver, gold and gems. They had copper masks and caskets. Everything has energy from Eden.

The mound builders had giant elongated skulls, and their skeletons were eight to twelve feet tall. They were buried with arrowheads, bowls, jewelry, and smoking pipes. These giant Indians clearly had sacred traditions and ceremonies for life and death. These beings were known as elders to the Natives. They were respected but also greatly feared. For which they held special abilities and superior strength.

This creature is known to uproot trees and stuff them back in the ground upside down. The beast can launch rocks farther than a hundred yards. One female Sasquatch kidnapped a prospector and licked his palms and feet raw so he could not escape. These beings remain close to their ancestors' ancient altars, so Ohio of course remains a hotspot. Old Orange Eyes patrols Cleveland's river tunnels all the way down to Mansfield. Some say he is in the woods behind the Cleveland Zoo.

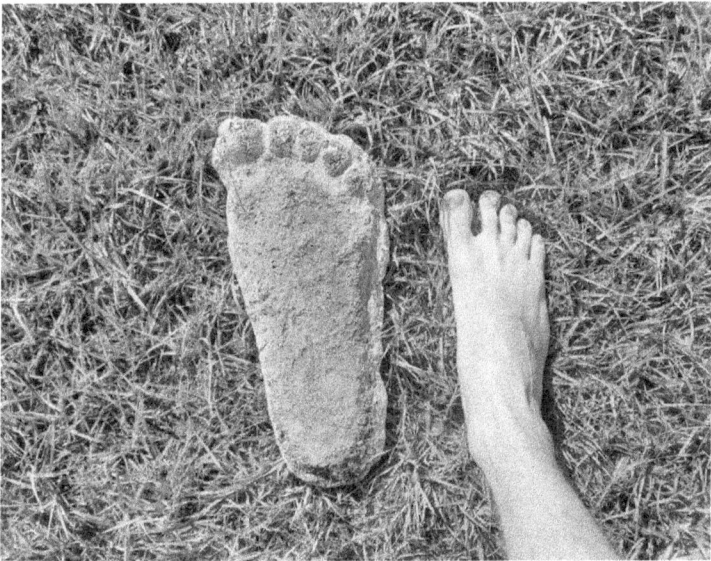

Footprint

Over the years, I have hiked many trails and spent many nights camping in the Bigfoot capital. Our fifth-grade trip to Mohican was full of Native American tales of titans and creatures in the surrounding area. We searched for arrowheads, and they showed us a giant in the rocks. It was a fossil of the gods that once roamed the ancient lands. We drank from Hemlock Falls and made sure to stick close to the group because the sightings of Bigfoot were high in the area. We canoed and kayaked, but the most dangerous thing we saw was a biker gang on rafts. Most of my camping was down in Salt Fork, and that's where I first encountered the Grassman.

A couple of summers before I visited the Ohio Bigfoot Conference, I had my own encounter down in Salt Fork. My parents were staying in a camper with my babysitter's family, while all the kids were outside in tents. We ran wild during the day, playing football and Frisbee, but when evening came, that was when capture the flag started. I was known to be stealthy, so my first idea was to flank them. I took off down a path in the woods, hoping not to be seen or heard.

I crept through slowly but heard something approaching, so I hopped behind a tree stump. I peeked around and saw my babysitter and his friends moving forward with the same plan that I had. I slowly creeped on as the leaves' crackling fell distant. I grew paranoid because I still felt like someone was nearby. As the seconds felt like hours, I wondered why they hadn't tried to tag me yet. It was getting darker by the moment, so I moved from tree to tree in the shadows.

No action yet, but I still felt the presence. I stopped for a breather and closed my eyes. When I opened them,

I saw a juvenile Bigfoot peeking around a tree through the moonlight. Her eyes caught mine, and it felt like time was frozen. There was an unspoken understanding of peace and an instant wish for a world where we could either switch roles or coexist as friends. I blinked, and she was gone.

I moved in toward the flag and freed the people in jail. They were able to grab the flag and head back towards our base. I went off toward the woods again. I heard cheering and commotion from a distance and knew that the babysitter had the flag too. And nobody knew where he was except me. I heard the leaves cracking and tackled him to the ground.

He fought back, flailing his arms, not expecting the collision. We tussled for a moment, when a tree cracked in half, crashing right toward us. That had us to our feet in no time. We looked into the darkness and heard my new friend's father pound his chest twice and let out a fearsome roar. It shook the ground, and we both took off toward camp. In the game, we came out on top, but I had fallen for the Grassman's daughter…

CHAPTER 9
OCTOBER AT MANSFIELD REFORMATORY
RICHLAND COUNTY, OHIO

T he Mansfield Reformatory is one of my favorite places in Ohio. The prison was used in *Shawshank Redemption*, *Escape Plan 3*, and Lil Wayne's famous "Go DJ" music video. There are bus tours, overnight stays, and even tours led by former inmates themselves. During the Halloween season, they use part of the former Civil War training camp as a haunted house with the scariest fright actors in the state. The gothic castle is now home to a music festival and has been featured on countless ghost-hunting shows. Mansfield was a halfway point between my house and my grandparents' farm, so the "Most Haunted Place on Earth" was destined to be on my path.

It was October, and I was with my buddy Monk. He was a childhood friend and roommate of the kid on CNN who threatened Kent State. We used to explore Princess Ledges after dark and had had a few odd encounters. We'd seen an older lady looking for her cat, and had heard many strange sounds from the trailer park. We'd explored the Cascade Park waterfalls and the carvings at Worden's Ledges when we were old enough to drive. Wolf told him about our night in Helltown, so he'd had his eyes on the reformatory for a while.

We chiefed a few Ls and reminisced on our times on the road. We'd visited the Ford Theatre and heard the story of how John Wilkes Booth assassinated Abraham Lincoln. We'd stood in the rain for the changing of the guard at the Tomb of the Unknown Soldier after seeing JFK's grave. We had been told stories about phantom soldiers and horses on the Gettysburg tour. And both of us laughed when we remembered the story of the Killbuck Swamp Killer that our camp counselor had told us at Mohican in fifth grade. Monk had a few of his own crazy stories about Erma's house and living with the Kent State Menace. Before we knew it, we had arrived.

I had done the daytime tour when I was younger but had no clue what to expect with this. The haunted tour was forty-five minutes long and filled with sixty-plus movie-ready actors hiding around in the shadows to scare the shit out of you. We parked the car and lit up one of the roaches. After a couple of puffs, there was a huge bang on the window. I thought it was the cops and almost lost my cool. But instead, it was a masked man who looked like the backwoods mutants from *Wrong Turn*. He stared at us for a while but then chose to run after a vulnerable family that just parked. We walked towards the gothic castle and got ourselves two tickets with glow sticks, meaning the actors could touch us.

For a half hour, I peered into the windows and imagined Andy Dufresne looking back at me. We ripped Monk's dab pen and made friends with a couple named Riley and Rustin. Rustin told us about the graveyard that was on the grounds and a story of a teenage boy who was beaten to death in the basement. They were both from Asheville and had traveled all across the world, looking for scares. Riley told us about vampires in Romania, the yeti in the Himalayas, and a couple of stories about her childhood home in the mountains. They reminded me of my adventures in Asheville with my aunt Gloria. We offered them our pen, and they offered us colored pieces of paper. We put them under our tongues and waited patiently for our turn to enter the prison.

Twenty minutes later, I was feeling pretty funky, and it was our turn to enter the haunted house tour. We laughed with our dilated eyes and ducked under the artificial spiderweb blocking the entrance. Our glowing wristbands were cool to our eyes and also meant that the monsters were allowed to get a little physical. Riley and Rustin led confidently while Monk and I took our time feeling out our surroundings. There were plenty of perfectly timed jump scares. The masked actors did a great job of hiding around the haunted corridor. The ghouls loved to push us around and try to separate groups of people. I knew from watching *The Houses October Built* that these fun haunted houses could turn dark very quickly. In my current condition, I was not ready for anything like that.

Halfway through I began peaking and absorbing all the energy that had swept through the prison during the past centuries. I was vulnerable. I went through a trap-door and was now alone. I heard inmate screams and even felt one pull me back into a cell. I fought out of it, but I could barely breathe. The next thing I knew, Monk was pulling me up to my feet, laughing. He made it seem that I was with the group the entire time and imagined the entire thing. I took my glowing wristband off and finished the rest of the haunt with no problems.

Speechless from the prison, we needed some water and smoke. We said our goodbyes to Riley and Rustin, then entered the endless maze of automobiles. We zigzagged between the cars and finally found where we were parked. We smoked a joint in silence, staring at the belly of the beast. Monk pulled out slowly while I rolled another, listening to some Strange Music. I searched under the seat for a lighter, and when I picked my head up, I had to do a double take. I felt the car slowing down and thought I saw a woman running from the woods.

A moment later, Monk was on the side of the road, and my window was rolling down. The woman was frantic, asking, "Where's the prison? I need help! They want my treasure!" Her white dress was covered in leaves, mud, and blood from the cut on her hairline. We offered her a ride, but she ran off in the direction of the prison when we pointed to help. We drove the speed limit home and were thankful to finally see our drive-way. We told his mom about our experience, and she almost dropped her glass of wine when we told her about our ride home. She'd had a similar experience in high school and said, "You boys met the ghost of Phoebe Wise!"

CHAPTER 10
SURVIVING MOUNDSVILLE PRISON

THE WEST VIRGINIA PENITENTIARY

A cross the road from an Adena burial mound lies the most haunted prison in the Midwest. You may know it as Castle Rock from the Stephen King series or might have stumbled upon the grounds in *Fallout 76*, but this is usually a place that you want to stay far away from. With links to Charles Manson and many murders and executions on the property, the penitentiary is a haven for ghost hunters and dark tourists from all around the world. The Ohio River valley is no stranger to occult phenomena, and best believe that all the residents lock their doors at night, especially after the prison break and manhunt that left the entire region in shock forty years ago.

My grandpa would tell me that back in the day he used to swim across the Ohio River for fun with his friends. I couldn't imagine doing it unless I had to, like some of the escaped prisoners in '79. Fifteen prisoners overpowered the short-staffed penitentiary and wreaked havoc around Moundsville. An officer was killed, and the town was never the same.

Across the street from the resting place of titans, the prison has executed over a hundred inmates and witnessed just as many unsolved murders within its walls. After catfishing next to the coal barges, we pulled our boat up to the Riverside Restaurant for their famous pizza and calzones. I went to the bathroom and found a flyer for a tour of the prison; tonight was the night.

I could see the castle in the distance, but we pulled beside the burial mound to pay our respects. I closed my eyes and tried to soak in the energy that had soaked the valley. There was definitely an odd feeling in the air. I imagined the mound builders flourishing in the OV, communicating with the gods above. I took my final gaze at the structure and headed towards the entrance.

Moundbuilder. Sun Worshipper. Ancient Ancestor.
(Face drawing)

We paid for our tickets and were handed a flashlight. The first half of the tour was guided, and the rest we were able to roam free. The guide explained how the prison was supposed to hold about 400 inmates but was required to hold about 2,400. The overpopulation led to riots and the spread of rapid sickness. They showed us a letter that Charles Manson wrote to the warden, requesting a transfer to be with his mother. The warden replied, "When Hell freezes over."

We crept through the cafeteria and entered Death Row. They showed us "Old Sparky" and nine pictures of the men who were electrically executed. We went towards the North Gate and saw a noose hanging where many men were hanged. I visualized mobs of people screaming and cheering while the guide described the time when an inmate's head popped off due to his weak neck muscles. His head rolled like a bowling ball to my feet, and I finally opened my eyes. I was sitting in the cell, staring at the carving in the wall. The gate was locked, and this didn't feel right. I looked around desperately for a sign of life, but I was alone. I shook my hands on the bars and let out a scream. I came back to consciousness, and everyone was staring at me.

Embarrassed and confused, I ducked off into the shadows, away from my family and the other tourists. I explored the recreation yard and ended up at the chapel. I was in a daze and ignoring most signs of instinct. A dark presence followed as I headed down into the Hole. I got turned around and started to get sick. I put my head down in the corner and gave myself a couple of deep breaths. After a moment, I felt a touch on my shoulder and heard a voice asking, "Are you alright?" I opened my eyes, expecting to see my cousin or grandpa, but it was a strange man, and he seemed to know me. We were doing a bid together. He passed me a cigarette, and I snapped back to reality when it touched my hand.

My sister found me in the hole and told me about a cold spot that they'd found in the dentist's office. I followed closely, trying to make sense of the strange occurrences. My flashlight flickered, and I gave it a good smack. Cousin gave out a quick screech and claimed he saw a shadow bolt across the pen. We moved slowly, peering at all the artwork in the Sugar Shack, with caution in every step. I heard whispering behind me and asked my cousin what he said. He just shook his head, and we did not stop until we reached our grandparents. We finished the tour and were finally out of the furnace. As I climbed in the Blazer, my grandma found a cigarette that fell out of my pocket. She said they hadn't made that brand in years.

CHAPTER 11
ASHEVILLE CASTLES

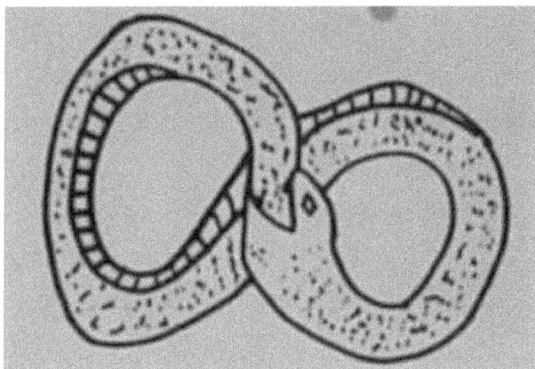

Sketch I did of an Ouroboros

A sheville is an imaginative gem tucked in the hills of North Carolina. With a rich history of art and theater comes the pain and dark places that inspire the emotional colors that now layer the groves of downtown. People from all around the world come to see the Biltmore Estate and walk the grounds that George Vanderbilt once tended. But the lucky ones get to see his ghost and hear his calling wife. Others come to hike the trails of the national forest and raft the white waters, but don't wander too far off the path! Daily ghost tours and a Bigfoot festival keep the residents and tourists informed of the local legends of Asheville!

There have been many different types of creatures that have been spotted in the Appalachian Mountains. Cherokee legends shed light on creatures in the forest and entities in the sky. There are still tribes of people that live off grid deep in the mountains, and many people credit the strange phenomena of the mountains to these groups. But the anomalies that have occurred stretch far past this wild race.

Hunters and fishermen have encountered Sasquatch hundreds of times over the years along the trail. And even more people have reported UFO sightings. But crawlers, pukwudgie, and aggressive dogman sightings are becoming more common with time. And that is a problem. Especially for whoever was driving with me in the car. I'm a magnet for strange!

Credible people have spotted enormous black wolves that were powerful enough to flip cars. Witnesses have reported werewolf-type creatures that have the ability to scale trees, cloak, and use mind control similar to the alien in *Predator*. Tracks, dens, and kills have been found by hikers. Bone-chilling howls, growls, and shrieks roar through the valley almost every night along the trail. Many people believe them to be from a pack of wolves or coyotes, but others think the skinwalker might be responsible.

Along Blue Ridge, a park ranger pulled over a family in a minivan for speeding. The woman driving was hysterical and pleading to the officer to allow her to keep driving. She said her car had been attacked while the family pulled off the road to take a picture. The ranger could see claw marks torn into the side of the van.

The twenty-five-year veteran went back to his Crown Vic and was checking out her license and paperwork. He heard the woman scream, then drive off immediately. He was confused and looked in the rearview mirror and saw a massive wolfman. He grabbed his shotgun and watched the creature jump over the railing.

The man ran back to his car and reported a bear on the highway. The car was suddenly attacked on the roof and being torn by the monster's sharp claws. The park ranger was inches from being eaten and finally let off a shotgun shot, and the beast ran off. The hardened vet was visibly shaken up but incredibly lucky. But not everyone shares the same fate.

On that note, my grandparents were bringing the four grandchildren to Panama City for spring break. We made this trip every year. We heard all about the Mothman, the yahoo and the snallygaster that roamed the bush as we drove through the West Virginia Mountains. We talked about the movies *Wrong Turn* and *Rest Stop*, joking about what could go wrong if we wandered off these same highways. We took many pit stops to fully embrace the road trip south.

We stopped in Roanoke to fill up our tank and ran into a creepy little kid in the gift shop. The git told us that a group of a hundred colonists vanished from an island of the same name without a trace. He looked like he came from a different world... He ran off with his dog into the woods, and I didn't think of it again until I heard the premise of *American Horror Story* season six.

After hours on the road, the sun was going down, and we drove to the top of the famous Brown Mountain. We stopped at Table Rock and Wiseman's View to see if we could catch a glimpse of the mysterious glowing lights that have been driving the region crazy. The phenomenon was covered in an *X-Files* episode and has been the topic of many other TV shows, movies, songs and books. There was definitely unique energy up there, but for the most part it was just peaceful to feel the air cleansing my soul.

As the family packed up the car, I wandered down the path to go to the bathroom. As I started to go, I felt like I was being watched and heard something large rustling in the leaves down the cliffside. With all the alien abduction stories in the area, my heartbeat rose. I imagined myself being clawed and thrown off the cliff to my death. I looked up into the sky and saw an orange glowing light. But I was not scared; it felt familiar. I knew it was protecting me, and the noise stopped. I got back to the car and wrote it down in my journal. Ten years later, I encountered that same light with Bird in my backyard. I look forward to encountering it again and logging in my journal for a third time.

After what felt like a lifetime, we finally made it to Asheville to visit my grandpa's sister, Gloria. We went to a Tourists game and kayaked near the famous Biltmore estate. We played cards and hunted the creek for snakes. I played tennis with Gloria, and she told me about the art district downtown and the famous ghost tours. After dinner, we went joyriding in my aunt's convertible red Mercedes. Gloria took us out for ice cream and asked us if we wanted to see something cool. So of course we were excited for the surprise.

She drove us deep into the winding roads, and my sister asked if we were almost there. The car whipped to the side of the road. We were very confused, and she pointed above. There was a huge stone bridge that led to a gothic Van Helsing-esque castle called "Zealandia". My aunt lit a cigarette and told us to keep our eyes peeled for a ghost named Helen. She yelled to watch out for snakes!

We got out and walked around, scanning the cliffside for activity. Stones rolled down the rock wall as the wind blew. My cousin Nicole had had enough, and Aunt Gloria had had enough fun. We pulled into the garage, and before I even took my shoes off, I heard my aunt scream, "Who left their muddy handprint on my hood?" I looked at Zac, and he looked me in my eyes and whispered, "Helen."

Decades later, I have returned to Zealandia in meditation and dreams. I'm constantly trying to figure out what secrets lurk below the stone castle. The cloud of vibration in Asheville is only comparable to a couple of places I have experienced in my days. The energy is similar to the Grand Canyon, Dealey Plaza, and, of course, glimpses of Terrestrial Paradise. I look forward to returning for a Bigfoot conference with a table full of books and merch! I would go back to the Biltmore too!

CHAPTER 12
SILVER MOON AND THE SNOWMAN
LAKELAND, FLORIDA

T he Silver Moon Drive-in Movie Theatre is one of the coolest landmarks in all of Central Florida. The famous sign, delicious treats, and obscure titles bring a cult following to the sacred ground. Lakeland is known for the beautiful lakes, monster gators, and the famous Munn Park, but its land holds the soil intact of many legends. The prestigious Polk Theatre, Terrace Hotel, and Lake Mirror would soon be my stomping grounds, but the Silver Moon will always shine bright in my memory.

My house sold in November, and I had a football tournament scheduled for January. I stayed with a friend and did tile and grout work to pay for my stay. When the new year hit, I knew I needed a change. I took the passenger seat out of my Ford Contour and built a bed. I planned on living at parks and marinas, sleeping in my car. Luckily on my adventure, I met some like-minded people, and the rest is history.

The first people I stayed with on Couchsurfing ended up becoming my family. They accepted me with open arms and gave me a place to stay when I needed it most. I'm forever grateful for that. I envisioned moving out of state thousands of times during my childhood, and some of the visions were spot on. Others were a total surprise. I always wanted to work at a pub and live above it. This might be the closest I get to that.

I never could have imagined the journey that awaited me in Central Florida. The group was part of a punk rock band that just wrote a musical. They were accepted to perform in the Orlando Fringe Festival and were looking to complete their cast. Luckily for both sides, the couch potato rolled right on in. I came through midweek, and the entire cast met each other Saturday, so naturally I was in and on the ground floor.

My roommates were rock stars, actors, and true Floridians. They all had a checkered past but would give up the shirt off their back for someone who needed it. They all had interesting stories, and I got to dive into each of their personal lives. I was everyone's escape. I was from the other side of the country, so they all felt a certain level of comfort with me. It led to many adventures. It was magical that we all had the show as our primary focus, and we each brought something unique to the table. We spent nights customizing costumes, designing logos, and reading lines. Our diverse backgrounds were a perfect melting pot for a multicultural show. The project was a perfect outlet for our creativity, love and anger.

The group was bonded on a deep spiritual level as well. Starting the very first day, we gathered for intense group meditations. We stretched our faces, cracked our bones, and lost ourselves in trance. We burned incense, candles, and listened to ambient sounds. We put together certain variables to achieve unique energies in our ceremonies. I was pretty sure I envisioned all of this happening back home, doing psychedelics during the Blood Moon. I tuned into my own archaic vibrations.

We witnessed some incredible things. We felt like we could control the flames and communicate telepathically.

Clouds of energy floated through the rooms, and there was always a feeling within the walls that could never be fully explained. We experimented under our orange tree, in the middle of the street, and even in a graveyard. We channeled ancient energy and really pushed the boundaries of reality. Sometimes it was a lot to handle. Meditation and just everyday life, that is...

We met many interesting people and invited them to the punk house. Some joined our meditation sessions, but others just rocked out on the drum set. Many friends and family just wanted to come over and see a behind-the-scenes look at the show. They also wanted to taste the chaos and break some plates in the infamous "Glass Corner".

Our house was the headquarters for the production. We accepted people with open arms when they had nowhere to go. One of our members had a gang of people after her and stumbled in with stab wounds multiple times. Seeing that much blood and wounded flesh is something you really never get used to. Most of the time, that'd be my cue for a bike ride.

I loved riding past the haunted Terrace Hotel and around Lake Mirror. I always wondered what was behind the cages and below the Frances Langford promenade. I would smoke joints and imagine Blinky's reptilian adventures while passing his statue. It was my home away from home. Whenever I was missing Ohio, stressed about the show, or heartbroken about my girl, I'd take to the lake.

But when the lake wasn't enough, I went to the Moon. The Silver Moon was my haven, my perfect getaway. I got to relax for five hours and kick back to two movies. The pizza was incredible, and the hot chocolate was delicious. It was the only thing that truly felt like home. It was nice to get away once in a while. Sometimes all of it was just too much.

After I got ripped off in Tampa and almost killed on the highway, I called my friend Nate, fuming! I was pissed off and needed something to turn my luck around. He mentioned hitting up the drive-in theater after he met up with a friend to pick up a bag. The tension in my shoulders loosened up, and I told him I'd meet him there.

We were going to see *The Snowman* with Michael Fassbender in it. It looked like a scary strange independent movie. I loved Fassbender in basically everything he's done, so it was a no-brainer for me. The second movie was *Thank You For Your Service* with Miles Teller. I'm a big war movie fan, so it was a nice added bonus.

I pulled into the theater and realized I was extra early. I was struggling with my broken phone and was happy just to make it to safety. I parked my car and finished off a roach. I went to take a piss and explore the grounds. I bumped into a man in all black and noticed some gangs of kids along the back fence. As I gathered myself in the bathroom, I took a deep breath, admiring the wild voyage thus far.

I grabbed a hot chocolate and ventured back to my car. I lay back in my seat and watched the movie trailers on the screen. I sank into a trance and woke up in an empty parking lot. I crawled out of my car and started veering around the grounds. It was a ghost town. It felt like a dream, and I was in school with a test in front of me. I was in the wrong place at the wrong time.

Out of nowhere, the projector started, and an image began to play. It was an edge of a forest. I moved closer to the screen to see if I could make out any details. As I crept forward, I noticed something dark coming toward me out of the treeline. The image was blurry and crackling. I inched closer as the hairs on the back of my neck began to rise.

Now the strange anomaly was fully out of the forest cover and still slowly heading this way. I took my eyes off the screen and scanned the facility. I was still the only one here. A mist rose from the concrete, and an unusual vibe was blanketing the area. When I glanced back at the screen, the creature was crawling out of the picture and onto the pavement! My heart tripped into my stomach as I fell deep into the sunken place.

When the black creature completely entered my realm, it gained structure and doubled in size. This thing was now moving at a fair speed and closing the gap. It was oozing and sputtering with one thing on its mind. When my body thawed out, I took off running. I debated jumping the fence and booking it to safety, but I hopped in my car. I turned the key, but it wouldn't start. My heart was pounding, and the creature was getting close.

Sketch of The Snowman

I punched the steering wheel and beeped the horn as it slithered nearby. It leapt up on my hood and was staring me in the eyes. I broke eye contact and shook violently, pumping the brakes. Finally the car started, and when the engine roared, the creature expanded its mouth, and I could see nasty fangs and the inner organs.

I felt like I had a heart attack, and everything blacked out. I woke up to Nate banging on my glass. I almost had an accident in my pants, believing it was the police or even the monster itself. He laughed at me and asked what the heck was up. I told him I was exhausted and had just met the combination of an alien and Samara from *The Ring*.

I crawled into his car, and the movie started shortly after. *The Snowman* was one of the most confusing and strangely paced movies that I have ever seen. I only made it halfway through the second movie before I'd had enough. The creature from the dark side of the moon was the only thing on my mind. I truly wonder if that has ever happened to anyone else who fell asleep before the show started. I will forever look at my chapter in Lakeland as a very important step closer to the promised land.

CHAPTER 13
PROVIDENCE CANYON CREATURES
STEWART COUNTY, GEORGIA

n Georgia, there are bulldogs, falcons, and hawks, so only the brave can enter the woods. The Altamaha-ha is the cryptid of the state, but there are many monsters patrolling the dense uncharted lands of the peach capital. Fifty years ago, farmers' error created one of the most stunning American land formations east of the Mississippi, Providence Canyon. The little Grand Canyon has miles of stunning trails and a couple of mysteries hidden within the red clay. Since moving to the Panhandle, I knew I had to explore the terrain.

There are many legends in the tristate area. The Rood Dude lurks the swamps and woods in the region. The large hairy beast calls Rood Creek home and doesn't take too kindly to visitors. Two campers were attacked in their tent and forced out of the woods. They reported the sighting at a nearby gas station, and the rest is history. The Rood Dude has been spotted at Lake Eufaula all the way to Providence Canyon.

In nearby Columbia, Alabama, there is a legend of a giant ghost pig. It was on the front page of the newspaper and seen by more than a hundred people. They said it had red eyes and stood on two legs. The mayor had it run through him, and the town marshal quit after encountering it. This strange creature is still spotted to this day and strikes fear into local hearts.

Not far from Columbia, Huggin' Molly is the famous legend of Abbeville. After dark, the seven-foot-tall nightgowned figure would patrol the streets of the town. If you were out when you shouldn't have been, she would run up to you and squeeze you as hard as she could while she screamed in your ear. The sound of her piercing cries never leave the brain. She has been spotted many times and even has a restaurant named in her honor.

My friend Dean and I met at the Expendables and Through the Roots reggae concert in Tallahassee. He was with his mom and FSU girlfriend, and I was with my sister. He had a couple rolled up, and we had the lighter that we needed. We all hit it off and were drinking long after the show. Dean and his mom were from Virginia, and they had a long list of mountains and trails that they've hiked. He was a professional bodybuilder now but still wanted to stay active. He brought up Providence Canyon, and I immediately asked, "When are we going?" His mom said, "Next time I'm down here!" A couple of months passed, it was his mom's birthday week, and she was coming to the Panhandle after the KISS concert in Tampa, and we all planned to see the red rock.

After midnight, I finished watching *The Wind* after hearing a couple of Florida State film students wrote and produced the supernatural western horror film. I drifted to sleep and became the male version of Lizzy Macklin defending my homestead against demons inside and outside the walls. I fended off hordes of attacks and was starting to break through when I was suddenly knocked to the ground. I rolled and pointed my rifle in the direction of the collision. I could feel the heat from the beast's roar on the back of my neck. I locked eyes with the behemoth and pulled the trigger. But the gun didn't go off. I woke up as the ferocious hog took a bite out of my head.

Since I was up early, I decided to take advantage of the morning while Dean and his mom were at breakfast. I remembered my dentist told me ghost stories there at the community college and also at the university. I had to check them out! I had to see the place that I'd heard so much about. I pulled up to the Florida State campus and was hypnotized by the beauty. Doak Campbell Stadium stood tall while garnet and gold painted the campus below. I passed by fountains, trees, and many friendly faces. I was beginning to see many Greek letters, and I knew I was getting close. Moments later, there it was, the Chi Omega Sorority house, where Ted Bundy killed two sorority sisters forty years ago.

White Witch's Grave at Florida State University

I stood there, trying to tune into the energy of the place decades back, and suddenly heard a soft voice asking, "Wanna check it out?" In the blink of an eye, we were in the same hallway that Bundy crept through before brutally murdering the two sisters. He attacked three other women around town that night, but they were able to survive. After the tour, we smoked a joint, and she told me about a girl who got struck by lightning on the roof of Cawthon Hall who still roams the halls and takes showers in the middle of the night. She also mentioned the gravesite of the White Witch in the nearby Old City Cemetery. Bessie was a good one who cast spells of love and fortune. She still has many visitors to this day. When I heard the giant gravestone has an excerpt from Edgar Allan Poe engraved into one side, I knew I had to see it.

I got a text that Dean was almost ready, so I said my goodbyes. We exchanged Snapchats, and I told her I would be in town for the next good concert. I stopped by the cemetery on my way out and paid my respects to the White Witch. A gust of wind grazed my cheek as I turned back toward my car. I made another quick stop at the Velda Mound Park. It was daytime and peaceful. I sat for a while, soakin' it in. The mound was used as a fort by the Apalachee people in the 1400s. It is rumored that there are giants buried in the mound. During nighttime, people have heard a wolf howling and a group of

Indians sitting around a fire, enjoying themselves. I enjoyed myself, and minutes later, I pulled up to Dean's house, ready to go.

I had my guitar, a knife, and a couple rolled up for the ride. His mom had just gotten back from overseas and was telling us about all the new food and drinks that she had tried. Her mind was blown by all the hurricane damage; it was the first time she had been down since the Category 5 storm. She was taking pictures the entire time. She offered to drive after Dean almost swerved off the road, eating his weird meal prep for his bodybuilder diet. After two hours and a couple of stops, we were finally pulling up to the park. I should have guessed, Dean forgot his lighter. Luckily, I met two pretty local girls, Aurora and Harmony, who wanted to join along on our adventure.

We quietly passed by a wedding in progress and trekked up the red rock. The first canyon that we climbed was the most challenging. We fought up the steep terrain and settled in a spot that overlooked many of the other trails. I sparked up a cigarillo and passed it amongst us. We blew the smoke into the clouds and appreciated the bird's-eye view. After minutes of serenity, we heard a loud grunt from the thicket off to the side. I thought that maybe it was a deer or large man, but both the girls said, "Bacon," and were confident that it was a hog. I had just watched the Aussie horror film *Boar* the week before, and I didn't want to be torn to shreds by the pig or his tusks!

After the THC kicked in and we climbed down the canyon, I forgot about the grunt and began admiring the maze of the red rock. The ground had a constant flow of water, and below the tree canopy, the temperature was very cool. We took pictures and spotted a few large spiders and snakes along the creek bed. Hours passed on the White Canyon Loop Trail, and we decided to branch off and test the Backcountry Trail. This was an old logging trail that is very dangerous from the steep and rugged path. We each grabbed walking sticks and sparked up another. With each puff, the surrounding forest began to come more and more alive. We tossed the roach and continued our hike in high definition.

After a while, Dean's mom stopped us and said it would be getting dark soon and that we should start heading back. Of course, Dean and I wanted to keep pushing forward but stopped dead in our tracks when Harmony asked, "Remember that growl?" Aurora added, "You don't want to be out here when it's dinner-time." And they continued to tell us a story about the Canyon Creature, a descendent of the famous "Hogzilla" and the mud volcano "Wog". These trails were home to a wild boar that has grown aggressive and in size ever since being trapped in the basin when the land first collapsed. And we were on its land.

The monster has been shot, speared and poisoned, but still roams these trails as the alpha. This apex predator is fast, ferocious, and shows no mercy. It has attacked vehicles and hunted down family pets. The sun was going down, and the wildlife was beginning to settle. Dinnertime was approaching, and anything in those woods was on the menu. We were still a couple of miles away from the rim when we heard a tree fall down about forty yards down the ravine. Dean told us to keep going while he hesitated to see what had made the ruckus.

I led the girls up the steep slopes and turned back toward Dean when I heard him yell. Dean was now running full speed up the path, and I knew something was wrong. The girls took off sprinting, but I knew what I had to do. It was our only chance. We were still far enough away from camp that it could catch and hunt each of us down before we reached safety. Finally I caught a glimpse of the beast, and it was closing in on Dean. He zigzagged and hopped over fallen trees while the hog just barreled through like it had an EZ Pass of the forest. I waited until Dean was directly below me, and I launched a large rock. It timed up perfectly and smashed the boar right in its snout.

The hog shook its head violently and let out another loud grunt. The growl shook the ground below and made the rest of the hair on my neck stand up. The creature resembled a wild piloswine. The beast looked me in the eyes, and I reached down for another rock, but by the time I was ready to launch, the monster was out of sight. I caught back up to the group and was greeted with handshakes and hugs, but I was still focused on the task at hand. The creature could still be stalking us and planning a final stand. At this point, I was ready for Ted Bundy to pop out of the bush and bite us!

We picked up the pace and made it back to the rim just before the sun completely set. I turned around and looked back down into the canyon one last time and imagined the beast staring back at me, plotting his revenge. I lit the last L and gave the girls their lighter back before saying our goodbyes. On the ride home, we were happy to be alive. Dean used to tease me about Bigfoot and chupacabra, but after meeting the razorback, I think he will bring more protection and fewer jokes on the next journey. I know I'll be ready…

CHAPTER 14

FISHING WITH THE OCHEESEE WILD MAN

THE FLORIDA SKUNK APE

Headless boar. Possible Skunk Ape kill.

E ven with all the headlines, I don't think Florida Man has anything on the Skunk Ape. Though I'm sure they'd make a great team, I think his first thought would be to run if he encountered the Creature from the Black Lagoon face-to-face. The king of the gators and leader of the wild monkeys, the Skunk Ape is the apex predator of the swamp. Underwater or in the trees, this giant beast will sense you before you have any idea that you are not alone. After one was caught in the 1800s, the existence of this new species should be widespread, but is being kept under wraps for good reason.

I have interviewed over ten people who have encountered the Skunk Ape firsthand. I have heard of sightings from military veterans, fishermen, farmers, and even the Florida Wildlife Commission. Mysterious noises, strange smells, and tree breaks are just the tip of the iceberg. Dead livestock, orange glowing lights, and telekinesis abilities are where things start to get hairy.

Florida is home to many mysteries. There are pyramids in the Everglades, dinosaurs in the swamp, and Indian mounds almost everywhere. The Garden of Eden and Fountain of Youth both connect to the Bermuda Triangle and Devil's Den. Giant gators, boar, jaguar and python are the least of Floridians' worries when the Skunk Ape still patrols the swamps! The Sunshine State's mysteries go back much further than St. Augustine!

Although most encounters include being chased out of the woods and growled at, there have been multiple positive experiences with these ancient beings. The natives used to trade along the Trail of Tears with the species. One interesting modern tale includes a young girl in Ocala National Forest. She was badly injured far from camp and was bleeding out. She was losing consciousness when she was scooped by an "orange orangutan lady".

The young girl was relieved but also grossed out. She was being held up against the Sasquatch's breast. It smelled like sour milk and rotten animal stink. The child believed the mother was pregnant. She was dropped off right outside camp and forever thankful. There have also been people saved from drowning, pulled from under landslides, and protected from bears and other predators. The ancient one's original mission was to protect the forest and all its inhabitants. Even the humans...

It was early in the morning, and my mom and I were heading to Ocheesee Landing to do some fishing. It was a couple of months after we spotted ten-plus barefoot tracks in the mud that were six inches wide and much longer than my size thirteen shoe. We pulled up to the historic oak tree and started unloading the car. The nearby area is rich with culture, history and legends. There have been sightings of bull sharks, dolphins and giant gators below the water's surface and even more interesting things on land...

There have been sightings of thunderbirds, mountain lions, and a giant three-toed sloth. Clans of aboriginal people are still known to roam the state. The Clovis tribe are known as bog people and have different sized skulls than normal *Homo sapiens*. There have been a number of television shows and guided exhibitions across the river at Torreya State Park, and many interesting local stories come flooding through the cracks. Stacy Brown and his father filmed arguably the best thermal footage of Sasquatch in the region and that forever blankets a level of curiosity while I'm exploring.

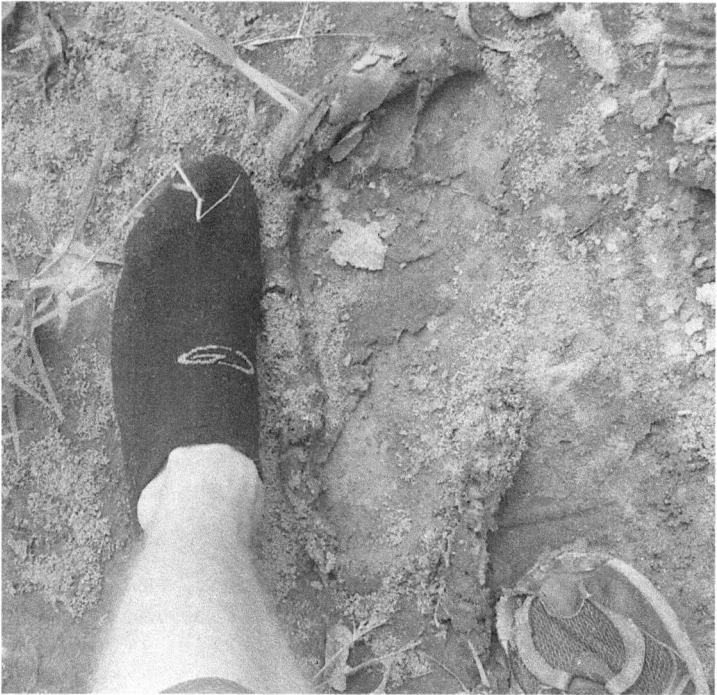

Giant Skunk Ape Footprint

Downstream, Arcadia looms near. The location is like no other. There are deep ravines, fossilized bluffs, dense jungle, and an area that resembles the desert. There have been ancient bones of saber-tooth tigers, mastodons, whales, and megalodon teeth the size of my hand found all along the riverbanks. The area is like no other region in Florida and very well could be the place that Adam met Eve. So a Bigfoot in the surrounding timber isn't too far on the strange side. The unique vibrations seep all the way down to the ancient pillars of this planet.

In the late 1800s, the small town on Ocheesee Pond was being terrorized by giant men in the night. After weeks of damaged equipment, stolen food, and dead farm animals, a group of local Civil War vets and Indian hunters took to the woods with guns, dogs and torches. They were able to track down and capture the wildman that was causing all the ruckus in the swamp. It was a large giant hairy humanoid creature. The human hybrid was taken to Florida State Hospital and was covered by all the newspapers along the east coast. It even appeared on the cover of the *New York Times*. Sadly the creature died three years later and is now buried over by where the golf course used to stand.

I was helping carry down the fishing supplies when I heard my mom calling my name. She was very excited and pointing to something on the ground. It was a fresh track! But it was not a deer or bear, it was something much larger. My entire shoe was able to fit in the large footprint. I took my New Balances off and compared the sizes. Unless Shaquille O'Neal was fishing the banks of the Apalachicola, this track was made by no man. The footprint was far too wide to be a human. There were about twenty tracks marching from the wood line into the water. I took pictures of the best ones, and then I settled in to fish. When I got home, I posted the evidence on a couple of cryptid forums, and the replies urged me not to go back to the location without a loaded weapon.

Weeks later, we returned to the landing to do some morning catfishing. My mom had told her father about the strange occurrence, and he bought her a handgun for protection. She had been practicing shooting targets in the backyard every evening since. I knew that if I posed no threat to the creature, I would most likely have no problems. But of course, just in case, I had my fishing knife for a last-second poke in the eye. But based on the bodies of the Russian students killed in the Dyatlov Pass incident, I would most likely be torn to shreds and fed to the alligators. After helping my mom get settled in, I went adventuring toward my spot.

All the best fishing stories I have heard at Ocheesee Landing center around one spot. The "Big Bend" is a haven for monster fish. The heavy current brings the bait fish in, and the powerful undertow keeps them trapped like minnies in a bucket. Right off the cliffside, the water dives to dark cold depths of at least eighty feet, and the caves in the rock go much deeper. There is no telling what kind of monsters lurk below. I lost my footing climbing the steep banks and decided to have my arm and legs scraped up by the sharp rock rather than ripped apart by the killers below. I moved with extra caution because that morning I felt something was watching me from the bluffs above.

I finally made it to the fisherman's chair and realized that someone had already beaten me to it. I smiled and nudged the sleeping tarantula from my spot. He was groggy but found a crack to crawl into. I got comfortable and threw my line in. After a while of no action, I decided to spark up a swisher and drift away for a bit. I imagined the Seminoles fishing these same banks centuries prior. I went deeper in my head and visualized Adam meeting Eve in this same delta. I was yanked back to reality when my bait was attacked and my rod was bending toward the depths. I jerked and hooked the beast! He put up a good fight and almost pulled me in the water multiple times, but after a strenuous battle, I finally landed the giant mudcat.

As I dodged the catfish's barbs, I called out to my mom to bring me the bucket. I wrestled with the monster and heard some rustling up above me. I peeked with the corner of my eye and caught a glimpse of something looking in my direction. I tried to remain calm and make it seem like I hadn't just locked eyes with the apex predator of this land. I could tell that he was very interested in the fish. Without any hesitation, after I got it unhooked, I chucked the fish up and over the bluff. My mom came around the corner, wondering what I was hollering for. I told her I'd caught a huge cat, and she asked where it was. I pointed to the top of the cliff and said, "It's his now." And before she was able to ask who, we heard a loud but peaceful howl, as if he was saying thank you. My mom dropped the bucket as we heard the creature run off into the thicket, leaving only our silence behind.

CHAPTER 15
MIDNIGHT AT BELLAMY BRIDGE
MARIANNA, FLORIDA

At the Bellamy Bridge

Back during my first October in the Panhandle, I was very excited to finally experience the haunted ghost tour around Marianna. With stops at the Russ House, a haunted church, and Civil War battle locations, the tour finishes up at the famous Bellamy Bridge. A local actress plays Elizabeth Bellamy and explains her story to the crowd. Her ghost has been known to visit the bridge, and she is not always too kind to trespassers. With rumors of Bigfoot and gremlins in the surrounding area, the tour was calling my name. Sadly, Category 5 Hurricane Michael obliterated the area, killed more than seventy people, and left thousands of others without electricity until the new year. The tour was cancelled, but the bridge still stood. The magnet still tugged.

Severe flooding and forest damage made it impossible to reach the bridge for months. But once the path cleared, I knew I had to find it myself. Two paranormal explorers with military backgrounds joined along after months of discussing local legends at the comic store and smoke shop. Dameco lived in Hawaii and was used to trekking through the jungle, while Ron grew up in these woods and seemed to know a little bit about everything. He served in Korea and Kuwait and had many stories. He thinks I'm a Marxist Communist, but we get along through our passion for cryptozoology. He has called me Karl for a while now, but after our night at Bellamy Bridge, I have a new nickname and a newfound respect for the mighty outdoors. She almost took my life on this unexpected night.

The skies were pouring, and Tattoo Rob, our fourth horseman, wasn't able to make it. But Dom had traveled from another time zone, and I'd waited too long, so the time was still now. We followed behind Ronnie, burning one listening to Joe Rogan podcasts, eager for the adventure that awaited us. I'd worked all day, so I was a bit unprepared. I hadn't eaten a full meal and was still getting over a weekend of severe dehydration after umpiring a softball tournament. Regardless, I carried on, not honestly thinking about it until my flashlight died a couple of hours later.

We arrived at the trailhead and followed Ronnie into the woods. Tonight was the perfect night by the ghostly standards. Elizabeth was most likely to be encountered on a rainy, calm night where a thick layer of mist covers the Chipola River like a blanket. The snakes were out, the gators were near, and the wild boar left tracks that even the rain couldn't wash away. Right away, we knew we were not alone out there. The red moon above illuminated the forest in a bloody way, letting me know that tonight would be a special one.

I read online that it was a short hike to the bridge. So after about an hour in the woods, and no river, I had a weird feeling. After the hurricane and severe storms since, there were trees and debris scattered in every direction. Ron and Dom both claimed the terrain was more rigorous than anything they'd encountered in the military. We kept moving forward, just hoping to run into the river, and then we would follow that to the bridge. My feet were now soaked from swamp water, and my clothes were drenched in sweat and rain. Dehydration was kicking back in, and it was becoming harder to breathe. My phone was dying, and we had no clean water. Dom finally checked the GPS and realized we were in a completely different location than we believed.

With all the fallen trees, it was very easy to get off track, but being on the completely other side of the forest didn't make sense. My heartbeat was starting to rise, and my head was pounding. I felt dizzy, but I had no choice but to carry on. Trees and paths were beginning to look the same, and it felt like we were going in circles. I've watched a lot of scary movies and always thought that was impossible. We trekked for a hard twenty minutes, fighting through branches instead of going around them, and we stopped in a clearing.

I lay on the ground while Dom checked the GPS and said we were in the same spot as before and just went in a huge loop. I couldn't believe it. I felt like I was in *The Blair Witch Project*. I no longer trusted my own judgment, and I felt like the guys were questioning themselves as well. I couldn't tell east from west; shit, I couldn't even find the moon in the sky. But really, where did the moon go? The woods were now much darker, and my flashlight was starting to flicker. I knew we were in trouble.

The flashlight died, and that was when a little bit of fear kicked in. I started to plan out building a shelter and fire to dry off our soaked clothes. My feet were starting to hurt. I was battling a bad ingrown toenail, and the swamp water made my feet pruney and sensitive, while the rocks and sticks tore them up from below. Luckily Dom's phone still had a battery charge and a decent flashlight, so I began to lead the way with that. Our plan was to head straight for the road and to go through and over the fallen trees instead of around them. It was the only way to ensure not getting turned around again. We would stop every couple of minutes to make sure we were still heading in the right direction. That was when we heard the wolves.

Leading the way was draining. My breathing pattern was poor 'cause that steadiness was going toward the path. My body was shutting down, and my mind was just trying to find fuel. I needed water badly, so the sticks and vines tearing up my legs were the least of my worries. I still had to keep my eyes open for creatures. I had to shine the light so the guys would have a target if we were in trouble. I heard something from behind Ron and looked backward, but I stumbled down a hill, through some branches.

I opened my eyes, expecting the guys to be laughing at me, but they were nowhere to be found. I wiped some blood from the back of my head and started looking for them quietly. I heard some movement up the ridge and saw a faint light through all the fallen timber. I move quickly towards it, ready to greet the guys. I ran to the opening, but lost the light. I heard some metal creaking in the wind, and I found the bridge. I was checking out the structure, and I saw a figure. I locked eyes with it and was instantly allured. It was her, and she already had me around her finger. She smiled and dived into the water. I took off towards the river, and the next thing I knew, I was being violently shaken. I realized it was Ronnie after I blacked out for a second.

The Forest People.

They were happy to find me. They were pretty sure someone else was in the forest with us and that we needed to get back to the car. I was able to ignore the migraine and get back on track. We moved as a unit and could finally hear civilization again. We muscled through the last mile and finally found some familiar territory. We reached the street and followed it back to the cars. There was a flock of ATVs filled with Confederate flags in the parking lot. We were weak, outnumbered, and just ready for a bottle of water at that point, so we hustled back into town.

We sipped, we smoked, and we said our goodbyes. We left in good spirits, but the dark skies turned blacker. We didn't realize that we might have been put under a curse. Ronnie almost hit a deer on the way home, Dom

114

almost had his car stolen, and I got pulled over on the way home in the last quarter mile. Since I was soaking wet and shaking from dehydration, they thought I was very suspicious and pressed me hard. I'd crossed the yellow line, avoiding hurricane debris and the usual garbage cans and dogs, but they thought I was drunk. I told them I just got back from Bellamy Bridge, which probably wasn't the smartest thing. Luckily, after a while, the lead officer recognized me from umpiring and let me go. He thought my name was Weatherspoon. No, sir, they now call me Pathfinder…

CHAPTER 16
EDEN AWAITS US
BRISTOL, FLORIDA

Edge of the old continent.

Twenty-seven of the twenty-eight trees in the good book and the birth place of Gopher Wood. The Garden of Eden trail is a true paradise. Listed as one of the most strenuous hikes in the state, the path is a journey through time and space. A strenuous adventure through valleys and Civil War forts, focus and determination is required. The sacred land bobs and weaves through thick forest and desertlike terrain. Keep an eye out for Adam, Eve and the Forbidden Fruit, but also mind the sand for the serpent.

My buddy Adam was visiting from out of town, and I had to show him the trail. We visited the Truman House in Seaside, Look and Tremble rapids, and my grandparents in Panama before our spiritual experience. We shot pool at the bars and ended every night on the beach, looking for crabs and spaceships. We grabbed water and turkey sandwich supplies before pulling up.

It was late afternoon, so the sun was beaming down on us. We packed our backpacks and grabbed a pamphlet from the main pavilion. I knew to stop pretty often and hydrate. The hike was no joke, and I knew from umpiring that the sun and heat exhaustion go hand in hand. I had almost passed out on multiple occasions and thrown up countless times until I only had stomach bile in my belly. I felt it coming again.

We slid down the cliffside to check out this plateau we'd scoped out. AC wanted to get a sample of sand and search for fossils. I went first and made it all the way to the bottom. The cliff of the ledge was another forty feet down into the river. I looked back up and saw that it was much steeper than we both had imagined. I yelled to him that he should stay up there because I sensed I would need some help getting back up.

He thought it was a better idea for us to be together. He slid down and was gaining a lot of speed. I dove to slow him down so that he wouldn't go off that second cliff. It would be a large plummet into the rocks or just the gator-infested waters if he was lucky. He took a look up and knew that we were in trouble. We hung out on the plateau and got our rock samples.

I climbed up first and worked up the cliffside on an angle upward. There were multiple close calls, and sand poured down the hill from every step that I made. I was sweating profusely, and my body was beginning to shut down. My head was pounding, and my legs felt like I had run a marathon. I was more than halfway up, and I knew that I only had one good shot at this.

I leaped toward a fallen tree and grabbed onto the branches. I climbed the base as it started to slide down the hill towards AC. Dust filled the air as I flipped off it. Every step I made was about four hundred meters' worth of effort and energy. One time around the track. I took a few more steps at an angle and got up to the plateau of the original trail.

I was standing in thick sand, and the edge of the trail was at about shoulder height. There was nothing to grab onto, and it was very steep behind me. I would have tumbled down and crashed off the cliff. I would have been bloody alligator bait in seconds. I'd made it 99% of the way, but this last part was the hardest. I dug into the cliffside, searching for a root. I found multiple, but they were weak and broke off instantly. Finally, I found one that might create some leverage!

I grabbed onto this root with my right hand and yelled, "Look out below!" I knew this was my best chance, and I didn't want to be stranded here overnight or have the wildlife patrol find us. I accepted that there would be a good chance that I might die if this root snapped, but it was my only option. On a three-second count, I'd pull with my right hand, push with my right foot, and grab for anything I could with my left.

On three, I wiggled and scratched in the dirt but luckily got back on the trail. I yelled out to Adam in joy with my back against one of the wooden signs. He started on his way up as I felt my heartbeat racing. I was breathing heavy and overheating. I felt like I was gonna pass out but was so thankful I'd made it up that mountain.

I grabbed some water out of my bag and slowly sipped it. I knew we had caused a commotion and grew terrified that a predator was lurking near. I was in no position to protect myself. I was completely vulnerable, and my best weapon was trying to climb down the cliff. We had definitely given off the vibes of an animal in distress. I could feel something looming near me.

Adam was struggling. He was tired and dehydrated. The cliffside was growing steeper by the moment. The sand was sliding down to the river. It wasn't looking good. I was thinking I would have to hike out of there alone and find some help for him. The idea of lurking predators raised the hair on the back of my neck. I rolled over and found a log from the bush line.

I tossed the wood in the sand toward Adam and hoped it helped with some traction. He gained some ground and was just about ten feet from the top. He crawled and cried and reached out his hand. I ignored the presence of the beast and tried to help my friend. He inched closer as the sand below his feet was giving out. He started to slide and luckily gripped my hand.

I put my left hand on his backpack and pulled him up while he threw himself forward. He made it up, and we both lay there in the dirt, exhausted. I knew something was close, but it hadn't struck yet, so hopefully it was just curious. Just trying to figure out what the rustle on the usual peaceful cliffside was. In the land of angels and gods, the nephilim and demons would be inevitably near.

We lay there for about ten minutes and started hiking back the way we came. I knew the path forward was too steep for our energy level, so we headed back toward the bluff overlook. The bench looked like a golden throne at this point in my head. I was delirious from exhaustion and dehydration. My knees were trembling, and I questioned if I would even have it in me to make it back to the car.

Each step that I made, I truly felt like I was going to collapse. I scanned the forest and noticed the baleful presence had evaporated. The forest was illuminated brighter, and I could hear the birds like I was one. I pushed forward with my mind, and somehow my legs were able to follow. I lost myself and realized that ominous force that was hunting us may have been protecting us.

Ancient Ancestor

We made it back to the bench and finished off our water. This was the final lap; we had to be efficient. We sat there for a half hour, regaining our energy, as the sun crept farther away from us. We did not want to be here after dark with no flashlights or supplies, but we simply didn't have the energy to start the trek back to the car.

As I lay back on the bench, I was beguiled by the overlook view. I surveyed the treetops and imagined the four rivers below. The berries and trees that could help us survive entered my mind. My mind was at ease. We had everything we needed out here. I was worried about water but lay next to the river. I feared for light, but it would be a full moon, and I knew the way. We would be okay.

A roar from across the river woke me from my head trip, and it was time to go. My battery was half charged, but that should be enough to make it back to my four wheels. We hiked slowly and just focused on our breathing. The sun was down, and the evening skies were beautiful. We stopped at a creek to wash our hands and faces. We were revitalized.

We climbed the steep hills and laughed about our close call. Our heart rate had steadied, and we finally were starting to feel like ourselves again. I sank back into reflection. I was now joined by my neighbor and his young son. We were moving at a solid pace when I stopped suddenly and threw up my hand. Right ahead of us was one of the deadliest killers on the face of the planet, the true villain of Eden. The deadly serpent. The diablo dialed in as our eyes dilated.

We crept slowly as the six-foot eastern diamondback snake held his ground on the path. One bite, this far out, would most likely be deadly. I moved to the left and picked up a long stick. I softly tapped it on the ground ahead of me and tried to make peace with the creature. We had been through enough and just wanted to make it back to our ride but would have to pass the gatekeeper first.

The tail rattled, and the tongue wiggled. The serpent had patiently waited this entire time. Ready to strike when we let our guard down. I was very fortunate to look down at that moment. If not, I'm sure I would have stepped right on its body and been struck in my leg instantly. I stared into the snake's eyes, and they pierced into my soul. The serpent read me. Medusa turned me to stone...

Memories of Erma's house and Moundsville flooded my emotions. I reminisced on my journey so far. Visions of hunting with my grandfather, traveling with my dad, and fishing with my mom were programmed in my mind. I retraced my steps with White Shoes, but dark clouds came looking in. I remembered getting the call about my sister's car crash. I could see her in the hospital bed with tubes coming out of her. It was horrific. My stomach hurt in pain. I was going to die right there, I was sure of it.

Nightmares of Helltown and the witch from the Cry Baby Bridge overtook everything inside me. I felt like I was trapped in a maze of Zealandia. This pounding in my head was nearly unbearable. I had no choice but to face my fears and my past head-on. The dark shadows dissolved as I broke the gaze with the serpent. I had been tested; I had been cleansed. I had been given a second chance.

We continued creeping to the left, and suddenly the

serpent slithered in the opposite direction. Our path was cleared, and we were granted access to the safe path. We were tested, challenged, and manipulated but stuck together moving onward. We were very thankful that we were still not stranded on the cliffside and even more grateful the Nachash let us pass.

CHAPTER 17
FINAL LAP

As we conclude our journey, we realize that a much larger expedition lies ahead of us. Everyday life may seem to have a plan, but our paths can be rerouted in the blink of an eye. As long as we remain positive and adaptive, we will survive. As human beings on Earth and souls in this infinite world, I believe in us. I believe

Bone of an ancient animal found in Florida

in myself, I believe in you, but I also believe in and respect the unknown.

We are but a speck of dust but also here in the flesh as our creator's image. Let's just treat each other right and try to locate the things that bridge us to the Gods. Never play the Midnight Man game! Embrace your nightmares so you never forget to keep dreaming! Please only play with Ouija boards with people who know what they are doing. They can be very dangerous.

There is energy we cannot see, beings that almost can never be found, and land we have not touched in a very long time. Antarctica is a 360° ice wall that surrounds the oceans. I believe there is land beyond the poles, and that's based on the testimony of a man who was awarded the Medal of Honor. The moon is a plasma and the same size as the sun. The other planets are celestial bodies fixed in the firmament. We can only reach them as spirits.

Aliens are truly extraterrestrials. Terra means land, and they are creatures that come from the extra continents. There are lands in the sky like Jack and the Beanstalk, underwater utopias like Atlantis, and cities under our feet like Ember. The worlds beyond the wall might hold other versions of you and me. Visitors from subterranean caverns and jungle paradise keep the new world on their toes. Imaginary borders keep us separated from the true core.

The truth being hidden leads to hometown horrors like Stoskopf and White Shoes incidents. Misery and terror are inevitable in this world, but society being brainwashed definitely acts as a catalyst. The government tests the land and the people; then they lock victims away in haunted cages. It seems we are all rats in an experiment. We are not being accurately warned about what's really out there. There is a plane of existence that doesn't get any recognition.

There is a world war going on right now. There is a war on information, a war on the spirit and soul, and the war against our creator. The battle of dark and light has been going on for a very long time, and we were all chosen to take part in the show. It is easy to choose what side of the line you want to be on, but to hold strong on your two feet is much harder. It begins with clarity.

Ocheesee Pond, Florida. Location of the Wild Man capture.

Monsters are real but so is heaven. If demons exist, then so do angels. If the devil is hard at work, then God must be doing overtime shifts because we have had many sunny days. Our minds can summon rain clouds, and our spirit weighs twenty-one grams. Energy is never created nor destroyed. It has always existed. Coincidence is the only thing to never exist.

Mermaids, fire-breathing dragons, and the angels in the outfield are all real. There are remnants of the old world in every direction. The bayous were carved by the titans, the pyramids cannot be recreated, and the way that Stonehenge was aligned required advanced technology. This all might sound like a sci-fi movie, but all films have roots in reality. Welcome to the matrix.

We are not in a computer program, but there are many Agent Smiths. Our world has meaning. We have a creator, and clearly they are working with more than x's and o's. The sun tells the time, the moon names the day, and the stars determine the year. The golden ratio stretches further than artwork, pinecones, and our internal makeup. We need to hold the seashell in our hand and look into ourselves. Mysteries and madness are right around the corner, so proceed with caution!

Until next time, remain safe and connect with me online. I have had the privilege of being interviewed on a bunch of different paranormal shows, talking about my experiences. Check me out on *Sparks of the Paranormal*,

Induced Fear, BigfootSociety, Hangar18 Radio, Squatchcast, Rare and UNusual, and many more cool radio shows! A few of my stories have been narrated on Dixie Cryptid, Swamp Dweller, Cryptids Canada, and Bigfoot Case Files. Check out my music under the alias cflynna! We are all energy! Embrace the Martian!

CHAPTER 18
LETTERS FROM FAMILY AND FRIENDS

Maryasiye

My grandmother's house in Ireland

Soooo… Your grandad's sister (Mau Flynn) told us that one day when she was very young (around 10 years old ish) she was told to do a 'message', e.g., go to shop, send a message to the neighbour, etc.), and on her way there she saw a fragile old lady with very long grey/white hair brushing her hair, sitting on a stall outside a specific neighbour's house (neighbour being named Mrs. Lynch)—she had never seen this woman before, and in those days everybody seemed to know everyone around the neighbourhood and village.

The next morning the news came that Mrs. Lynch had passed away and that the story is that the grey-haired lady was a 'banshee' that was symbolising that Mrs. Lynch was soon to pass away (old Irish folk law). This same woman was apparently never seen again, and our great-nan never believed her due to nobody knowing of this woman in the village! (But my nan, Mau Flynn, swore that the story was true!) x x x Each time we went back to Limerick, she would always show us the same house where she said to have seen that woman sitting on the stool!

———

Alex

Well, I guess my statement would be... I take a left onto Sunrise Oval off of Sleepy Hollow Road. As we pull in, we stop because we think a deer is crossing the road. When we looked though, it wasn't a deer, it was something on 2 legs that ran across the road faster than the average person could run. It ran up a hill in almost a gallop.

My guardian angels, Baby and Ben

Second story, I believe you were there, but we heard rustling outside my walkout basement, we looked out the window, and there were eyes like 5"5' to 6' looking into the window... taller than any known Ohio animal could stand.

———

Jake

Grassman sketch

Pulling into the Sleepy Hollow neighborhood, woods to the left, big field/hill to the right with a red barn at the top of the hill. As we're pulling in slowly, we see a figure crossing the street on two legs resembling a werewolf/bigfoot, bigger than a human, and as soon as it crosses the street, it dead sprints up towards the barn, running faster than humanly possible. Still feels like a dream...

———

Birdman

When we were younger, we used to go out in the woods by Kenski's house and just hike and BS.

My childhood home in Ohio

One night we got spooked by something and started running home... we stopped about halfway to look back because we heard noise from far away... all of a sudden a huge light lit up the entire woods for about 3 seconds, and then we never heard anything or saw where it came from... only time I can think... bolster it however you want.

———

Hannah

It was a cooler fall night in Chatham Township, and just like any other weekend night, a few friends and I were sitting around the fire, enjoying each other's company and having a few drinks. We were about an acre back from my friend Alana's house in her backyard, which was a typical hangout spot. We have never had issues with phone service, and we always connected our phone to a speaker and were able to stream music with no issues. Something this night felt off.

We all were sitting around talking, and we all brought up how something seemed "weird". We ignored it, shook off the feeling and continued to listen to music while a few of our other friends were driving around the four-wheeler. Randomly the music stopped playing, and my friend asked for someone else to connect to the speaker. We all checked our phones, and every single one of our phones had no service. We didn't really think much into it, but again a strange feeling. This has never happened before, and the area typically always had fine service.

An hour or so goes by and still no service. This is when we realized our feelings of something "feeling off" earlier in the night were validated. We saw two figures back further in the yard, a bit wooded area. At first we thought it was our friends that were on the four-wheeler but did not hear the four-wheeler. We started to call out their names with no response, but it seemed these two figures were getting closer. All of us got quiet and started to panic a bit when all of the sudden our two friends ran from the wooded area (no four-wheeler), claiming the four-wheeler broke down.

Sasquatch sketch

Here's when it got weird, the two figures were gone, and at this point we had not mentioned to our other friends on the four-wheeler what happened. They said they saw two figures and thought it was us coming to check up on them. When they realized it wasn't us, and they walked towards the figures, they mysteriously also vanished. We then all started to walk towards the four-wheeler, panicked at this point, and we heard the music BLASTING. How though when the phones had no service, and it wasn't music we typically listened to.

While in the wooded area, again, we all saw the figures, but then again they disappeared. The four-wheeler happened to start back up, and at this point we decided to go back up to the house. What we all witnessed is unexplainable and still gives me a weird feeling just talking about that night. Our phones also did not end up having service until hours later, at this point it was almost morning time.

———

Nate

As a young kid growing up, imagination was everything to me. From sliding down the stairs in a laundry basket, thinking I was escaping a base under attack, to starting world wars in my bedroom with GI Joes. People believe that children may see beings from other dimensions; or ghosts as some may debate; others would like to believe it's just their imagination. For me, on the other hand, [it] was far from imagination.

Deep sea fishing in Clearwater, Florida

While playing with action figures by the window in my grandfather's attic, my dad heard me talking to someone as if they were in the room with me. He thought it may have been me just talking as characters I was playing with. My dad then came into the attic to check up on me, and my action figures were on the total opposite side of the room, and I was standing by an open window. My dad then went on to ask who I was talking to. I proceed to tell him the man in the black tuxedo. My dad then asks where this man went. I told him that he had jumped out of the window.

Time has passed, and years later this story came up at a family function and that's when I learned that my great-grandfather died in the house I was in, and at his time of death, he was wearing a black tuxedo. To this day I believe I had an encounter with the ghost of my great-grandfather.

One morning while I was doing a little dog sitting at your dad's house, I thought it would be a great idea to watch *Paranormal Activity* and lay with the little pup. It was pretty early, so I was still really tired and dozing off. As soon as I started to slip under sleep, I saw a shadow in the corner of my eye, and Buddy went crazy. He was barking repeatedly and staring off into an empty doorway. Moral of the story, don't watch scary movies alone in a basement!

Tony & Adriana

On the road to the local library, Tony was seated on the passenger seat, there was a little swamp growing cattails nearby. He had noticed a figure standing in the water, until upon closer look, it was actually floating above the water. Shocked at this sight of a person levitating. The figure's silhouette seemed to be continuously moving. This figure had the shape of a person, but it was composed of thousands of gnats in a strange swarm above the swamp. It was facing the road, moving its arms slowly side to side as Tony drove down the road, the figure with its head now turned towards the car, staying in its place.

On left: Seth Breedlove from Small Town Monsters. He and I are both from Medina County in Ohio.

Adriana was fond of dolls as a young child and she collected porcelain ones. One particular doll that she liked was her musical doll that wore a green dress with her brown hair tied in a neat bun. She came with her own stand, and she was always sitting down rather than her other dolls who would be standing. She has a musical turner attached to her back, which would make her sway side to side whenever she played her tune.

Days turned to weeks when Adriana noticed that this doll would move on its own. Not too noticeable, the doll would always be in a different position in the morning. The doll was always facing Adriana when she woke up. Adriana noticed that on nights that she stayed up late, the doll would suddenly begin to play music, and each morning, the doll would be facing her no matter what position Adriana would put her in. The fondness she felt for the doll turned into weariness as she had a hard time avoiding the doll's stare. She then made the decision to lock the doll away so that she could sleep peacefully again.

———

Alli

We were riding on a four-wheeler on the main road in the middle of the day down from your grandparents' farm… Came around a bend and a big black cat leaped from the middle of the road and onto the hillside above us.

Age 3 with PePa showing me the farm

The hill is probably 10-12 feet high and it made the jump in one leap. Supposedly it's impossible for black panthers to live in Ohio, but I don't know what else it could have been. It was a huge black cat with a long tail.

————

Kalie

It was a Wednesday night in Mohican. I woke up and as soon as I did… I thought I was the last one up… considering I saw people walking around. I was still half asleep, so I didn't realize at the time I could see right through them. As soon as I walked right through someone, I realized I was seeing ghosts. Once they realized I can see them… they were all staring at me and intrigued. I can tell they were surprised that I can see them. They were all around my age. There were about 35-40 of them. So many faces watching me walk around the room.

My morning view

I was looking for someone to wake up to help me. I woke up to a girl, telling her I see ghosts. Please help me find a counselor. The first girl ignored me. The second one I asked helped. She led me to the counselor, and I told her everything I was seeing. The ghosts were all watching me tell my story. There were two right in front of me, "dead", hanging from the bunk bed from their necks. But most of them were "alive" and watching my every move.

One of the girls on the bunk bed where the dead people were hanging was reading a book. She put her book down just to listen to me talk about her. She was so pretty and looked very friendly. I can tell a few of them wanted to try and talk to me, but I was too scared at the time. But now I wish I did try to help them. They all seemed very nice but mostly just in shock as much as I was, lol. We were all confused and wondered why I could see them.

The counselor had me call my parents to tell them I was seeing ghosts, so I did at 5 a.m. They wanted to come and pick me up, but I didn't want them to. I didn't want to get made fun of that my parents had to come pick me up because of me seeing ghosts. So I told them I'm staying. I unfortunately still ended up getting made fun of the rest of the trip bc the word got around I saw ghosts and no one believed me except for one girl that helped me. I ended up sleeping in the teachers' dorm that night. I never cried that whole entire trip, but once I came home at the end of the trip… I let it all out to my parents in tears and was still in shock till this day.

Adam

5th grade Mohican school trip. I forget how long the trip was, but it felt longer than a few days. Just looking at the agenda made me sick to my stomach, and now I'm thinking to myself how I am going to spend a few nights with all these jerks (besides my friends obviously). Who wants to go anywhere in the middle of winter at that age (11) when there's no PS2, basketball hoop or football around, like come on. Not even a good enough hill around to sled down.

Tread lightly

The big picture of the trip in my eyes was to educate about the history around us and to try to have fun with more responsibilities than usual in your daily life. I wasn't having it. Seemed more like a prison system by how we were controlled. At least in prison there was no bedtime. Just a cold vibe from the start in a bad way for me.

My head just rushed with anxiety and an eagerness to

leave while having this cold, uncomfortable feeling of more life around us besides the people that we could physically see. At that age I thought every old place was "haunted", and maybe I was right. Games are already getting old by the 2nd day, the vibe is still a little uncomfortable for me, and I eventually get puked on that night to top it off. Talk about a backfire; I tried to make one of my friends laugh while he took a drink from his cup, and it took a turn for the worse. I've never in my life seen someone laugh, cough, hiccup and burp at the same time, but this kid pulled it off, resulting in him vomiting all over me.

So the coat's ruined, and the building is already cold as is, so I'm really happy by this point. The cabin had an old house feel to it that felt poorly insulated. The trip kept taking a turn for the worse as the hours went by, and people started to get sick, and now it's time for us to get ready for bed after a rough day. Someone didn't want us there. Being in the dorms was actually the best part of the whole night for me. We were able to get comfortable and hear intriguing ghost stories from this cool, younger "hippy" instructor while being annoying with our friends.

The stories were mostly about the Native Americans that once lived on the land that were still haunting the area. He also talked about how there was an asylum in the 1800s where the Indians once lived (most likely enslaved and/or forcefully put in the asylum).

While we relaxed and goofed off, we kept getting sunk into these ghost stories he was telling us about. They were very intriguing, and it was like he was doing his own spirit cooking through the stories he was telling. I had my own story to tell after that night, a spiritual one that I will never forget.

Once we all are asleep, I spontaneously wake up in the middle of the night while still in a dream state of mind like I was sleepwalking in a more conscious way. It felt like I was floating around the whole dorm room while moving at a faster speed than a walk and physically feeling nothing while my classmates kept slipping away. Then I remember uncontrollably heading towards the door that leads to outside like someone was leading me there. I hear someone say, "Hey, what are you doing?"

It's the "hippie", stopping me at the exit, wondering why I am trying to head outside. I don't even know if I ever responded to this poor guy, but I do recall just heading back gradually to my bunk while still in the same state of mind. My visual ends with me heading back to my bunk, seeing 3 of my close friends acting just as bizarre, talking in their sleep to hippies while he's trying to figure out what the frick is going on with these kids. I vividly remember hearing and seeing all of them be incomprehensible while trying to talk to him in their sleep. Then I finally fall back to sleep. So was I being taken outside by some spirit(s) or was my spirit taking me outside? For what reason? Did some other being want me to leave the dorm? Sounds like I took some psychedelics in 5th grade, right? Wrong, but it did somewhat have the same feeling as a deep psychedelic trip as I learned through my later experiences in life.

The time to wake up finally arrived, and I'm approached by a "hippie" telling me that I was sleepwalking last night. I played it off like I didn't know that I sleepwalked, but I did know. My spirit had woken up fully to express itself that night, or another spirit took full control of my body to lead me to their perspective in an unexplainable way. This trip was a drug-less mystery during my younger years when I think I might have been woken by the Mohicans. I used to sleepwalk here and there before the trip to Mohican. I never sleepwalked again, but life is a dream so…

Years later, you and I had a strange occurrence at a golf course. We had a secret spot that was shown to me through mutual friends where you have to walk through the woods and someone's backyard to get through. A peaceful night with the herb being passed. Starts to get dark, and we make the decision to head back to the car. Our sense of direction goes a little once we go into the woods, and the sun completely disappears, and we have nothing but a flashlight on one of our phones, and we get spooked because we spot a light that looks like a flashlight so I know I was thinking cop. But I still don't know what it was. Sleep well & Dream Forever.

Into the Abyss / Mexico Beach

ABOUT THE AUTHOR

Connor Flynn is originally from the coast of Lake Erie and now resides in the Florida Panhandle. His love for outdoors and investigative journalism has led him down many paths of strange and unusual things. Flynn has appeared in films "Zillafoot" and "The Void Cat" and hosts a horror themed podcast. Catch Connor in the swamp or on the screen, he stays active in the field always waiting for a scream!

Visit him at his YouTube Channel below and on other social media platforms.

YouTube: https://www.youtube.com/ channel/UCvcN_fkxz1wtjgwibEtF6qQ

instagram.com/bigfootanonymous
tiktok.com/@bigfootanonymous
facebook.com/cedrick.diggory.501

ALSO BY CONNOR FLYNN

Big Brother, Bigfoot